Jane Lady Coke, Mary (Cotton) Eyre, Ambrose Rathborne

Letters to Her Friend Mrs. Eyre at Derby

1747-1758

Jane Lady Coke, Mary (Cotton) Eyre, Ambrose Rathborne

Letters to Her Friend Mrs. Eyre at Derby
1747-1758

ISBN/EAN: 9783744692656

Printed in Europe, USA, Canada, Australia, Japan

Cover: Foto ©Thomas Meinert / pixelio.de

More available books at **www.hansebooks.com**

LETTERS

FROM

LADY JANE COKE

TO HER FRIEND

MRS. EYRE

AT DERBY

1747—1758

"Letters bring things more home, and represent them more to the life, than either Annals or Lives."—BACON.

EDITED, WITH NOTES,

BY

MRS. AMBROSE RATHBORNE

LONDON:
SWAN SONNENSCHEIN & CO., LIM.
PATERNOSTER SQUARE
1899

Authors and Works consulted and quoted:

Horace Walpole, Lady Mary Wortley-Montagu, G. Selwyn, Lady Hertford, Walford, Jesse, "Beauties of England and Wales," "Glover's History of Derby and Derbyshire," "Cox's Derbyshire Churches," "Hutton's History of Derby," and other genealogical, historical, biographical, and reminiscent books of the period.

EDITORIAL NOTE.

ERRATA.

Page 17. For George III. read George II.
  „ 51. ⎫
  „ 52. ⎪
  „ 56. ⎬ „ Winchelsea „ Winchilsea.
  „ 82. ⎪
Index ⎭

The originals, as well as the miniature of Mrs. Eyre which is here reproduced, are in the possession of my father, the Rev. Rowland German Buckston, of Sutton-on-the-Hill, Derby, who is the representative, on the maternal side, of the eldest of the four Cotton co-heiresses, amongst whom the Sleigh and Cotton estates were eventually divided.

I am obliged to Mr. and Lady Katherine Coke for their permission to reproduce the pleasing portrait of Lady Jane Coke; also to Mr. St. David M. Kemeys-Tynte for kindly supplying some information and facts relating to the Wharton family.

FLORENCE A. MONICA RATHBORNE.

SUTTON-ON-THE-HILL,
1899.

Horace W:
   Lady F
Wales," "Glover's History of Derby and Derbyshire," "Cox's Derbyshire Churches," "Hutton's History of Derby," and other genealogical, historical, biographical, and reminiscent books of the period.

EDITORIAL NOTE.

In editing these letters I have endeavoured to give a history and explanation of the places, events, and persons mentioned therein, by quoting extracts, as much as possible, from contemporaneous authors, newspapers and periodicals.

Unfortunately many letters are missing, and those preserved apparently form only a fragment of the actual correspondence.

The originals, as well as the miniature of Mrs. Eyre which is here reproduced, are in the possession of my father, the Rev. Rowland German Buckston, of Sutton-on-the-Hill, Derby, who is the representative, on the maternal side, of the eldest of the four Cotton co-heiresses, amongst whom the Sleigh and Cotton estates were eventually divided.

I am obliged to Mr. and Lady Katherine Coke for their permission to reproduce the pleasing portrait of Lady Jane Coke; also to Mr. St. David M. Kemeys-Tynte for kindly supplying some information and facts relating to the Wharton family.

FLORENCE A. MONICA RATHBORNE.

SUTTON-ON-THE-HILL,
1899.

I am Allways Dear M.rs Eyre's
 Affect.t Friend
  & Humble Ser.t
   I. Coke.

INTRODUCTION.

The Wharton family, of whom Lady Jane Coke was the last surviving representative, derived its surname from a "fair lordship" upon the river Eden, and traces its descent from Henry Wharton, of Wharton in Westmoreland, living in the reign of Henry V. Another ancestor, Sir Thomas Wharton, was governor of the town and castle of Carlisle, in the reign of Henry VIII., and successfully resisted an incursion of the Scots, putting them to rout, and making captive the Earls of Cassilis and Glencairn. He marched into Scotland with Lord Dacre, and was at the taking of Dumfries; for which, with other eminent services, he was created Baron Wharton and summoned to Parliament in 1545.

Lady Jane Coke was the eldest daughter of Thomas, fifth Baron and first Marquis of Wharton, whose father had been a staunch Puritan and Parliamentary partisan in the time of

Charles I. This nobleman, who was esteemed a profound and eloquent statesman, devoted himself zealously to accomplish the Revolution, and is said to have composed the first draught of the invitation to the Prince of Orange, and was created by Queen Anne, Viscount Winchenden and Earl of Wharton. A few years later he was advanced to the dignity of Marquis of Malmesbury, and Marquis of Wharton, and also made a peer of Ireland as Baron Trim, Earl of Rathfarnham and Marquis of Catherlough. He filled with great *éclat* the high appointment of Lord Lieutenant of Ireland, and took Addison with him as secretary.

The Marquis of Wharton had inherited two estates through his mother, the heiress of the Goodwyns; Winchenden, and Wooburn, both in Buckinghamshire; and the former he made his chief residence, effecting considerable improvements in the ancient manor, and its surrounding grounds, which at that time were considered as the finest in the county. On the attainder of his son, Philip Duke of Wharton, the Winchenden estate was sold to the famous Sarah, Duchess of Marlborough, from whom it descended to the present Duke of Marlborough. The old mansion was pulled down at the close of the last century and the materials sold, only a small portion of it remaining, which was used as a hunting seat. Wooburn was not neglected, for Lord Wharton is said to have expended £100,000 in altering the grounds belonging to the Manor House, which was surrounded by a moat, and retained its ancient character of feudal magnificence. The gardens as improved by the Earl were in that age highly celebrated, and are reported to have been in a line of terraces on the side of the hill, which has since been converted into pasture. The manor was very large and the apartments spacious. The gallery was 120 feet long, and contained the very celebrated collection of portraits of the Wharton family, which were afterwards purchased by Sir Robert Walpole, and subsequently sold by his grandson, amongst the famous Houghton collection, to the Empress Catherine of Russia. This mansion was taken down in 1750 after the death of the Duke of Wharton, and the materials disposed of for £800, the estate itself being sold to John Marse, Esq.

Lord Wharton's first wife was Anne, co-heiress of Sir Henry Lee, of Ditchley, Oxfordshire, but by that lady he had no issue. He married secondly Lucy, the daughter of Adam Loftus, Lord Lisburn, and grand-daughter of George

Brydges, Lord Chandos, by whom, at his death in 1715, he left issue a son Philip, created Duke of Wharton in 1718, an elder daughter, Lady Jane, the writer of these letters, and another daughter, Lady Lucy, who married Sir William Morice, a Devonshire Baronet, and died in 1738.

The life of Philip, Duke of Wharton has been written in detail by Jesse, by Walford, and recently by Robinson, and constantly recurring remarks about him are contained in letters by persons at this period, so that it will be only necessary to mention a few of the salient features of so eccentric a career, commencing with every advantage that extreme cleverness, great wealth, and position could give, and closing, bereft of all, in an exile's grave.

Philip was born in 1698, and married in March, 1714, when in his sixteenth year only, the eldest daughter of Major General Holmes. The marriage was performed by a Fleet parson, and was the first of the long series of escapades for which the young nobleman became afterwards so notorious. The young wife was said to be a person of "extraordinary education," and she appears to have preserved through all her troubles a blameless character. Her husband deserted her shortly after their marriage, partly, it is believed, at the instigation of his father, who disapproved of the match so much that it is said to have hastened his death, which certainly occurred soon afterwards. Two years later, and while yet a youth, Philip was created an English Duke; his influence, and the talents he had already displayed, no less than his avowed Jacobite tendencies, having probably made him an object of uneasiness to the new Government. The young Duke squandered his large fortune in the wildest profligacy, but appears soon to have repented of his abandonment of the Duchess, and to have been afterwards guilty of no worse neglect than keeping her in seclusion in the country. In Parliament his Grace attained to the reputation of an able and eloquent speaker, and his speeches against the Ministers were delivered with much effect; in the instance of the South Sea affair Lord Stanhope was so excited by one of these tirades that, in replying with extreme warmth, he burst a blood vessel and died. The Duke at last openly espoused the Jacobite cause, fled to the Continent, was created by the Pretender, Duke of Northumberland, and continued, much to the disgust of his new friends, to indulge in those eccentricities which rendered him notorious throughout Europe. He was attainted for high treason and his property confiscated. The Duchess died in London at her house in Gerrard Street soon after his flight, and the Duke married at Madrid, Theresa O'Neill O'Beirne, Maid of Honour to the Queen of Spain, the daughter of an Irish officer in the Spanish service, with whom he wandered about Europe for some time in an almost destitute state. He died in 1731, aged thirty-two, at the Benedictine Convent, and is buried in one of the aisles of the church belonging to the Monastery of the Franciscans de la Puebla at Rens, nine miles west of Tarragona, in Spain. At the close of the last century the traveller could dimly trace the name of the Duke inscribed on a small slab, which possibly now is entirely effaced. His Duchess soon after his death came to London, probably to claim recognition from the Government, as the late Duke's estates were producing an income in excess of their obligations. If this was her purpose she does not seem to have been successful, and died in 1777, and was buried in the ground attached to the old Parish Church of St. Pancras.

On the Duke's death, all his honours, excepting the Barony of Wharton, independently of the Attainder became extinct, which Barony is in abeyance (should the act of Attainder be repealed) between several families. His vigour of talent, and strong impropriety of conduct have been finely described by Pope in his Moral Essays, commencing,

> " Wharton the scorn and wonder of our days,
> Whose ruling passion was the lust of praise."

Lady Jane Wharton was born in 1706, and married 3rd July, 1723, at the age of seventeen, John Holt, of Redgrave, Suffolk. His uncle, Lord Chief Justice Holt, a Privy Councillor for twenty-two years, whose integrity and uprightness as a judge was celebrated by the author of the "Tatler," under the noble character of "Verus," the magistrate, bought Redgrave from the Bacons, and on his death without issue in 1709 the property descended to his heirs.

Lady Mary Wortley Montagu, writing to her sister, the Countess of Mar, in 1721, mentions the coming marriage as follows :

" Lady Jane Wharton is to be married to Mr. Holt, which I am sorry for, to see a young woman that I think one of the agreeablest girls upon earth so vilely misplaced. But when are people matched ? "

The marriage, however, did not take place till two years later, and no doubt it met with the approval of her brother, the Duke of Wharton, as it absolved him of his responsibility and afforded his sister better protection than he was likely to be able to give, as the parents, Lord and Lady Wharton, had both died within a year of one another in 1715. Lady Jane, notwithstanding her brother's extravagances and eccentricities, seems to have continued on affectionate terms with him till his death, and to have done what she could to save him from the effects of his own folly, and to preserve what was left of the family heritage. Mr. Holt died in 1729, and in 1733 Lady Jane married Robert Coke, of Longford, in Derbyshire, Vice-Chamberlain to Queen Caroline, and a brother of the first Earl of Leicester.

The Cokes became possessed of the Longford estate in Derbyshire by the marriage of Clement Coke, the sixth son of Lord Chief Justice Coke, with the co-heiress of Alexander Reddish, of Reddish, in Lancashire. The Reddish or Reddiche family had themselves obtained the estate by marriage with the heiress of Dethick, of Newhall, a family who held the property through marriage with the heiress of the ancient family of Longford, and who had been the owners of Longford from very early times.

Clement Coke was succeeded in 1619 by his

elder son, Edward Coke, created a Baronet in
1641, whose younger son, the third Baronet, died
in 1727, and the Baronetcy then expired, but the
estates passed by will to Edward Coke (eldest
brother of the first Earl of Leicester), who on his
death without issue in 1733 bequeathed them to
his brother Robert, Lady Jane's husband. One
sister, Carey, married Sir Marmaduke Wyvil,
Bart., and died childless, and the other sister,
Anne, married Major Philip Roberts, of the
Horse Guards, and the son of this marriage,
Wenman Roberts, on the death of Lady Jane's
husband in 1750, succeeded to his uncle's property,
and became the owner of Longford; and took the
surname of Coke, calling himself Wenman Coke.
He married a daughter of George Chamberlayne,
of Hillesdon, Bucks, and in 1759 on the death of
his other uncle, the first Earl of Leicester (whose
only son Viscount Coke had predeceased him),
inherited his, Lord Leicester's, extensive Norfolk
estates as well. Wenman Coke's eldest son,
Thomas William Coke, of Holkam, for many
years Member of Parliament for Norfolk, was
created Earl of Leicester of the second creation
of that ilk.

Longford Hall, where Lady Jane spent the
chief part of her second married life, is a fine

old mansion of red brick with stone facings, surrounded by an extensive and well-wooded park and beautiful gardens, those in the front of the house being laid out in the formal style of the last century.

The tower at one end of the old hall was pulled down about a hundred years ago, and the house has been considerably altered and modernised since Lady Jane's time, although the south or garden front remains of the same size and length.

Lady Jane appears to have been upon very friendly terms with her Derbyshire neighbours during the time she lived at Longford, and as the Cottons of Etwall were amongst the most influential of her nearer acquaintances, it was natural that some social intercourse should have existed between the two families. The special friend of the writer of these letters was the eldest Miss Cotton, Mary, afterwards Mrs. Eyre, and a close friendship existed between the two for many years, in spite of constant changes in the circumstances of both.

Longford remembers its former inmate, by a fanciful and comparatively modern tradition, and Lady Jane is now known as the "White Lady," and she is supposed to haunt her old home seeking for a lost finger of her left hand, as it will be observed that only four fingers are visible in the graceful portrait which is reproduced by permission of the present owner of Longford. The reader will be amused at this fable upon further acquaintance with Lady Jane through her letters, and will agree that she was a most unlikely sort of person to become a ghostly visitant. The painting was never quite completed, which accounts for the unfinished details of the hand. Perhaps Mr. Coke's death may have been the cause of this, as the picture represents Lady Jane at about the period during which she resided at Longford and was the queen of the county society of Derbyshire, for after her husband's decease, when the place passed to his successors, with whom she appears not to have been on the best of terms, she took a final leave of Longford, but her portrait remained there amongst the rest of the family pictures.

The pleasant expression in the painting seems to justify Lady Mary Wortley-Montagu's eulogium of Lady Jane that she was "the agreeablest girl on earth," and her letters to Mrs. Eyre, often written hurriedly and unreservedly, in varying circumstances, will be found to be wonderfully free from spiteful or ill-natured expressions about her fellow-creatures; although owing to her evident sense of humour she now and then indulges in a few caustic remarks, she does not show any signs of vindictive malevolence, even upon those occasions when she considers herself to be suffering unnecessary and undeserved humiliation.

The letters are all written in a beautifully clear and firm handwriting, on large, thick sheets of gilt or silver-edged paper; they are merely friendly and chatty letters, containing social items, fashions, news, and gossip, in which the names of various well-known people of the day occur, and they do not pretend to the literary merit of some of the more studied letters of this epoch, but manifest rather the simple and easy elegance of style of an educated and cultured woman of the period.

To modern ideas, the uncertain spelling, the liberal and erratic employment of capital letters, even in the midst of sentences, and grammatical errors such as "you was," may appear strange, but we must remember they were indulged in, and sanctioned by all the well-educated and most literary characters of the 18th century, namely Pope, Addison, Walpole, Mrs. Delany, &c. Therefore, in order that the letters may be read with greater facility, I have eliminated the frequent and unnecessary capitals, modernised the spelling, changed the invariable "y*e*" into "the," and occasionally corrected the punctuation.

It must not be forgotten that Lady Jane lived at a time when the coarsest of jests passed as wit, and sharp vituperation as smart repartee; the absence of both, in these letters, is the more remarkable when it is considered they were written to amuse her country friend, and contained accounts of the principal events going on in the gay world around her.

After Mr. Coke's death, Lady Jane spent most of her time for the next few years between London and Windsor, paying occasional visits to friends in the country, and to Tunbridge Wells and Bath, for the benefit to be derived from taking the waters. She then bought a house at Sunbury on Thames, and resided there until her death in 1761. She is buried in the Parish Church of Sunbury, where there is an elaborate monument to her memory, now unfortunately entirely screened and hidden from view by the organ. She left her large fortune to Miss Anna Maria Draycott, who afterwards became Countess of Pomfret.

Mrs. Eyre, to whom the letters were written, was the eldest daughter of Rowland Cotton, of Bellaport, in Shropshire, and Etwall, Derbyshire, who represented Newcastle-under-Lyme in Parliament from 1710 to 1715.

The Cotton family is traced from the reign of King Henry II., when Sir Hugh Cotton, Knight, of Cotton, in Shropshire, and his brother and heir, were ancestors of the Cottons of Cotton, Alkington, and Bellaport.

It was through Mrs. Eyre's mother, who was Mary, daughter and co-heir of Sir Samuel Sleigh, Knight, of Etwall and Ashe, Derbyshire, by Elizabeth Harpur, his third wife, that Etwall Hall and a portion of the valuable Sleigh property came into the Cotton family. The Sleighs were an old Derbyshire family.

Etwall Hall is a picturesque old house said to date from the 11th century, but the present building is of a later period, and the front is faced with stone brought from Tutbury Castle. The gardens were laid out in the quaint Dutch style by Rowland Cotton, Mrs. Eyre's father.

The small engraving of Mrs. Eyre is from a miniature evidently painted at a later period than that in which these letters were addressed to her, as Mrs. Eyre survived Lady Jane Coke a considerable number of years. It is to be regretted that no portrait of her exists contemporaneously with that of her distinguished friend.

Mrs. Eyre's husband was Henry Eyre, of Rowtor. He served as High Sheriff of Derbyshire in 1723. He married firstly Elizabeth, daughter of Sir Hickman Willoughby, and secondly Mary Cotton, of Etwall. By his last marriage he had no issue, but by the first he had one daughter, who married the Earl of Massarene.

Dr. Cox, in his "Churches of Derbyshire," gives the following account of the Eyre family, of which Henry Eyre was a representative :—

"They were an influential and powerful family in the Peak, where they possessed considerable estates. The founder of the family was named Truelove. He was at the Battle of Hastings, and seeing William of Normandy unhorsed, with his helmet beaten down over his face so that he could not breathe, pulled off the helmet and assisted him to mount his horse again. The Conqueror said : 'Thou shalt hereafter from Truelove be called "Air" or "Eyre" because thou hast given me the air I breathe.'"

After the battle the King called for him, and being found with his thigh cut off, William ordered him to be taken care of, and after his recovery gave him the lands in the County of Derby in reward for his services. The seat he lived at was called Hope, because he had *hope* in the greatest extremity, and the King gave him the leg and thigh cut off in armour for his crest, which is the crest of all the Eyres in England.

Most of the Eyres remained Catholics, being staunch to the old creed; but another branch, the Eyres of Rowtor, the descendants of the Eyres of Hassop and Rampton, became Protestant; it is not quite clear when they became possessed of the Rowtor estate in North Derbyshire, but they seem to have resided there for several generations. Thomas Eyre, who died in 1717, by his will left his body to be buried "in my chappell lately by me erected near my mansion of Rowtor," and he made his kinsman, Henry, the second son of Gervase Eyre, of Rampton, his heir, on condition of his constantly residing at Rowtor Hall (which had been recently rebuilt), where he was to maintain "a good house of sober hospitality." This condition does not seem to have been entirely complied with as Mr. Eyre resided principally in Derby.

LETTER I.

This letter is the first of the series written by Lady Jane Coke to Mrs. Eyre. The correspondence commences before the latter was married and while she was still Mary Cotton, living with her parents at Etwall Hall. It was usual to address all unmarried women as " Mrs.," and Mrs. Hannah More, who died in 1833, was the last single lady so designated.

The figs most likely came from the fig-trees growing against one of the old red brick garden walls at Etwall, and from the southern aspect the fruit would be sure to ripen well.

A "mobb" was a morning cap or head-dress, which continued to be worn until the end of the reign of George II., and no doubt Lady Jane was giving her young friend the benefit of her experience and taste, and had evidently undertaken to make up a becoming headgear for her.

To Mrs. MARY COTTON, at Etwall.

Dear Madam,

A thousand thanks for the best figs I ever tasted; Mr. Coke says he never eat better in Italy. I really take it extremely ill you should make any excuses about sending the mobb, which shall be made up as well as my servant and I together can do it, but you must give me leave to put it upon one of my caps, for yours won't do; as soon as it is finished I will send it.

Mr. Coke and I beg our compliments to Mr. and Mrs. Cotton, and believe, Dear Madam, I shall always be glad to execute any commands of yours, being

Your most obedient

J. COKE.

Friday.

•

LETTER II.

Since the previous letter the marriage of Miss Mary Cotton to Mr. Henry Eyre had taken place. The Miss S. Cotton mentioned in the postscript was Hester Salusbury Cotton, a little niece of Mrs. Eyre's, and the daughter of her younger sister, Elizabeth Abigail, who married Sir Lynch Salusbury Cotton, Bart., of Combermere, Cheshire, a descendant of the younger branch of the Cottons of Cotton. This little lady seems to have lived with the Eyres, and to have been a great pet of Lady Jane as well as of Mr. Coke, being constantly alluded to as "Madam Sal:" in subsequent letters.

Dear Madam,

Mr. Coke desires his compliments, and we shall be extremely glad of yours and Mr. Eyre's company here on Tuesday next. As I shall have the pleasure of seeing you so soon, I will only add that I am with great truth, dear Mrs. Eyre,

    Your affectionate,
      Humble Servant,
          J. COKE.

Longford, Sunday evening.

I shall be very glad if you will bring Miss S. Cotton with you, and beg our humble service to her.

LETTER III.

Sir William Stanhope here mentioned was Member of Parliament for Berkshire, being one of the four sons of the third Earl of Chesterfield, all of whom had seats in Parliament.

The Eyres at this time lived in Derby, which was about six miles distant from Mrs. Eyre's former home at Etwall. As the journey to London was then both expensive and tedious, not only did families in the neighbourhood of country towns resort to them for gaiety and shopping, but many possessed town houses in which they resided during the winter season.

The Eyres lived at Babington House, a fine old gabled Tudor mansion which formerly belonged to "the ancient and opulent family of Babington of Dethick," one of the first in the county, who erected the building many centuries ago, and made it their residence. The last of this unfortunate race was Anthony Babington, who lost his life, with others, through adhering to the unhappy Mary, Queen of Scots, against Elizabeth, and the family and the fortune sank with him. The house was one of the meeting-places of the so-called Babington conspirators, and stood on the north-west corner of Babington Lane. The ancient stone gateway was ornamented with the arms of the Babington family, sculptured in stone, supported by "Baboons" upon "Tuns." The hall was wainscoted with oak; in the panels were various devices, and baboons upon tuns carved thereon, the same being a play upon the name of Babington.

This old house, where Mary, Queen of Scots once slept, has been pulled down, and all trace of it has disappeared, and the site is occupied by modern buildings.

Mrs. Eyre, Derby.

Dear Madam,

I shall be extremely glad of your company, and will call on you next Tuesday morning and bring you to Longford. Mr. Coke bids me make his compliments and say he should be very glad to see Mr. Eyre at the same time, if he is not better engaged.

Believe me always, Dear Madam,
Yours sincerely,
J. Coke.

Sir W. Stanhope left us this morning. My compliments to Mr. Eyre.

Longford, Friday, September the 30th.

LETTER IV.

Lady Jane being a woman of fashion, and more often in the habit of visiting London, was naturally regarded as quite an authority on dress, and the subject was evidently frequently discussed between her and Mrs. Eyre, from whom the latter obtained hints and patterns, appreciating the former's wider experience and maturer opinion.

Chatsworth was at this period in the possession of William the fourth Duke of Devonshire. The present magnificent building, erected by the celebrated fourth Earl and afterwards first Duke of Devonshire, took the place of what was even then considered a fine structure, and entitled to be ranked amongst the wonders of the Peak, having been built by the celebrated "Bess of Hardwick," the wife of Sir William Cavendish, and who afterwards became Countess of Shrewsbury.

The Pole family lived at Radborne, where their descendants the Chandos-Poles still reside. The Squire at this time was German Pole, who unsuccessfully contested the borough election of Derby, in March, 1742, when Viscount Duncannon, son-in-law of the Duke of Devonshire, was elected. Mr. Pole complained of "undue influence" having been used, and attempted to set aside the election, for which purpose the Mayor, several of the aldermen, and a great many burgesses, set out for London to attend the House of Commons at the hour appointed to hear Mr. Pole's petition. A special messenger however overtook them at Market Harborough from the Duke of Devonshire, acquainting them that Mr. Pole had withdrawn his petition, whereupon they returned to Derby.

In June, Mr. Pole gave a great outdoor entertainment near his seat at Radborne, " to the burgesses and others of his supporters at the late election, at which there was great plenty of provisions and liquor ; nearly 500 persons sat down to dinner. The Squire, attended by several gentlemen, dined also in public with them."

There were several families of the name of Ward in the neighbourhood.

Dear Madam,

I send you with this, the pattern of the hood and cape you desired, and hope if you wear them it will be for ornament, and not be forced to wrap up, from the pain in your face, which I shall be glad to hear is quite gone.

Mr. Coke went to Chatsworth yesterday, and returns on Sunday. I know no sort of news, therefore will not take up more of your time, than to beg you will make my best compliments to Mr. Eyre and Miss Cotton and always believe me,

Yours sincerely,

J. COKE.

Longford, Friday morn.

I have just heard the whole family from Radbourn dine to-day with Mr. Ward ; imagine the bustle poor Mrs. Ward is in.

LETTER V.

The two friends now appear to be on more intimate terms, as Lady Jane does not address Mrs. Eyre as formerly, "Dear Madam," and commences the more familiar appellation which she afterwards usually continued, and her way of signing herself has become more affectionate, although she never discards the "humble servant" which was the invariable custom at that time, and of previous periods.

Mrs. Eyre has evidently been describing the social disagreements of Derby, and how the lack of male partners necessitated the ladies dancing with one another at the Subscription Ball alluded to, which was called an Assembly.

Glover, in his "History of Derby," writes :—"The old Assembly-room in Full Street, Derby, was opened in the year 1714; there are accounts of the expenditure to the year 1751, during which time the assemblies were conducted by the following Lady Patronesses :—Mrs. Pole, Lady Pye, Mrs. Coke, Mrs. Wilmot, Lady Atkins, Mrs. Godwin, Mrs. Chambers, Mrs. Bayley, Mrs. Fitz-Herbert, Mrs. Eyre, Mrs. Mundy, Lady Every, who evidently took the quarters in turn, and kept their accounts with great regularity. Under their patronage the assemblies were well attended, and the funds increased, but from 1741 to 1752 Mrs. Barnes was the sole patroness, and during these eleven years she appears to have exhausted the funds, keeping her accounts very irregularly, and never passing them until she resigned in 1752, and made the following curious entry in the account book, which shows how pointedly the distinctions of society were maintained at the time.

"'Aug. 4th. Delivered up the Assembly-room to the Right Honourable the Countess of Ferrers, who did me the great honour of accepting it. I told her that trade never mixed with us Ladies. A. Barnes.'"

The following are the quaint and interesting rules of the Derby Assembly at this time, and several of these printed notices are still extant :—

RULES
To be observed in the Ladies' Assembly at Derby.

1. No Attorney's Clerk shall be admitted.
2. No Shopkeeper or any of his or her Family shall be admitted except Mr. Franceys.*
3. No Lady shall be allowed to dance in a long white apron.†
4. All young Ladies in Mantuas shall pay 2s. 6d.
5. No Miss in a Coat shall Dance without leave of the Lady of the Assembly.
6. Whoever shall transgress any of these Rules shall be turned out of the Assembly-room.

Several of the above-mentioned Rules having of late been broke through, they are now Printed by our Order and signed by Us, the present Ladies & Governors of the Assembly.

ANNE BARNES.
DOROTHY EVERY.
ELIZABETH EYRE.
BRIDGET BAILEY.
R. FITZ-HERBERT.
HESTER MUNDY.

* Mr. Franceys was the Worshipful Henry Francis, Mayor of the Borough, an eminent and noted apothecary, greatly esteemed by many of the nobility and gentry, who often visited him, and was particularly remarkable for the grand entertainments he made on all occasions.

† Beau Nash, the great authority on fashion, could not tolerate these white aprons at assemblies, and on one occasion at Bath stript the Duchess of Queensberry of the apron she was wearing and threw it on to one of the benches. So little was this resented

Mr. and Mrs. Barnes lived in Green Lane, in the Parish of St. Werburgh's, Derby, by the side of the brook that runs through the town, and inhabited a very good house, bought of Mr. Green, who built it.

In connection with the Derby races there is an account of Mr. Philip Barnes's black mare, Moll Hackabout running a match with Colonel Gerey's grey mare Cassandra, for £100 a-side. One heat eight miles, each horse to carry twelve stone. Mr. Barnes's mare won.

"There was very good sport, the concourse of people was very great, there was abundance of coaches, several of them drawn by six horses, and 'twas tho't to be as large a meeting as at the last Nottingham races."

A ball followed at the Assembly-rooms on Monday night, and another at the Virgin's Inn on Tuesday night.

On a hatchment on the North wall on St. Werburgh's Church, Derby, are the Barnes Arms.

Mr. Stanhope, whose death is here mentioned, was the Hon. John Stanhope, the third son of the third Earl of Chesterfield; he was a Lord of the Admiralty, and Member for Derby from 1736 to the time of his death.

The fireworks about which the whole of London were at this time talking were to take place on April 29th, 1749, the thanksgiving day for the peace of Aix-la-Chapelle.

The apprehension that the site for the erection of the

---

that the good-natured Duchess acquiesced in his censure as he causticly remarked, "None but Abigails appeared in white aprons."

Pope's lines upon this incident are as follows :—

"If Queensberry to strip there's no compelling,
'Tis from a handmaid we must take a Helen."

fireworks was dangerous was fully sustained, as will be seen by the descriptive extract of what happened, taken from the *Gentleman's Magazine* of that date.

"The structure in St. James's Upper Park, or Green Park, begun on November 7th, was only completed on the last day. His Majesty George II. and the Duke of Cumberland attended by the Dukes of Montague, Richmond, and Bedford, and several others of the nobility, were at the library to see the fireworks. Soon after six the band played, and at half-past eight 101 cannon placed on Constitution Hill were discharged, and the grand display of fireworks commenced, but within the hour a portion of the structure had been burned to the ground, and the remainder was only saved by the workmen and carpenters cutting away the burning spars. His Majesty distributed presents to those most diligent in stopping the flames. By eleven o'clock the whole pavilion was illuminated, and continued so until two or three o'clock in the morning. The display was a very magnificent spectacle, and a general girandole of 6000 half-pound rockets, headed with serpents' rains, and stars surpassed all imagination in the beauty and greatness of its appearance. The Royal Family retired at twelve. The festivities did not pass without several accidents to those letting off the rockets, and one young lady had her clothes set on fire, but owing to prompt assistance escaped with only having her face, neck, and breast a little scorched, and one arrest is chronicled, for the designer of the building, whilst it was in flames, drew his sword and affronted the Controller of the Ordnance and Fireworks; he was quickly disarmed and taken into custody, but discharged the next day on asking pardon of the Duke of Cumberland."

The *Daily Advertiser* of this date gives an idea of the lavish display that took place, and enumerates the number of pieces intended to be fired as follows:—

Air balloons, 87; honorary caduceus, girandole, and other rockets from 4oz. to 6lb., 10,650; gerves or wheat-ears, 260; pots d'Aigrettes, 180; fountains, 160; pots de brin, 12,200; cascades, 21; wheels, 136; fixed suns, 71; marons in battery, 5000; lances, 3700; serpents, 130,000; figured pieces, 28; regulated pieces, 21.

Horace Walpole, however, condemns the show, which he writes "by no means answered the expense, the length of preparation, and the expectation that had been raised; indeed for a week before the town was like a country fair, the streets filled from morning to night, scaffolds building wherever you could or could not see, and coaches arriving from every corner of the kingdom. The merry and lively scene, with the sight of the immense crowd in the park and on every house, the guards, and the machine itself, which was very beautiful, was all that was worth seeing. The rockets, and whatever was thrown up into the air, succeeded mighty well; but the wheels, and all that was to compose the principal part, were pitiful and ill-conducted, with no changes of coloured fires and shapes; the illumination was mean and lighted so slowly that scarce anybody had patience to wait the finishing."

As so many exaggerated reports were afterwards spread of the reckless extravagance and immense cost of these fireworks, it was considered necessary to publicly state that a sum of £14,500 covered all expenses.

Rejoicings and firework displays also took place on

Thanksgiving Day at Derby, as well as in many other country towns.

Lady Caroline Pierpont was the daughter of the first Duke of Kingston by his second wife, and half-sister of Lady Mary Wortley Montagu, and was married to Thomas Brand, of Hoo, Herts. Horace Walpole, in a letter of the year 1754, written to Sir Horace Mann, thus writes of Mr. Brand:

"Mr. Brand, a very intimate friend of mine, whom I believe you have formerly seen in Italy, is just set out for Germany on his way to Rome—I know by long and uninterrupted experience that my barely saying he is my friend will secure for him the kindest reception in the world from you; it would not express my conviction if I said a word more on that head. His story is very melancholy: About six or seven years ago he married Lady Caroline Pierpont, half sister of Lady Mary Wortley (Montague), a match quite of esteem; she was older than he, but never were two people more completely, more reasonably happy. He is naturally all cheerfulness and laughter; she was very reserved, but withal sensible and faultless. She died about this time twelve month of a fever, and left him with two little children, the most unhappy man alive. He travels again to dissipate his grief: You will love him much if he stays any time with you."

Sir R. Atkins was the son of Sir Henry Atkins, of Clapham, and brother of the wife of George Pitt, who was in 1776 created Baron Rivers of Strathfieldsaye. He died unmarried in 1756, and the baronetcy became extinct.

Horace Walpole, writing about Fanny Murray and Sir R. Atkins, remarks: "It is the year for contraband marriages, though I do not find Fanny Murray's is certain. I liked her spirit in an instance I heard t'other night: she was complaining of want of money; Sir Richard Atkins immediately gave her a twenty-pound note. She said, "D—n your twenty pounds! What does it signify?" clapped it between two pieces of bread and butter and ate it."

A poem called "Essay on Woman," by Wilkes, commenced "Awake, my Fanny," meaning Fanny Murray, who after an erratic career eventually married a Mr. Ross, and died in 1770.

I think myself very much obliged to you, Dear Mrs. Eyre, for your letter—all the news you tell me. 'Tis hard out of two assemblies you have at Derby people can't agree to make one good one. Surely the men are rather impolite, or ladies would not be obliged to dance together. I never heard of a more melancholy meeting. The news we received yesterday of poor Mr. Stanhope's death shocked as well as surprized us extremely, for we had never heard of his being ill, nor was he longer confined than a fortnight; they say his illness was the gout, and imagine he hurt himself by living too low, which I always feared he would; as to Mr. and Mrs. Barnes, I have heard nothing of them since I saw you. If I was in her place I should be very glad to get rid both of the management of the Assembly and the money. I wish I could tell you any news in return to yours;

every letter I have is so full of the fireworks that I am tired of hearing of them. It is now apprehended they will damage the houses in both St. James's and Park places, and even break the windows in the Queen's Library, where the Royal Family are to be, so there must be some alterations in the scheme. Abundance of weddings talked of. Lady Caroline Pierpont to Mr. Brand, they say is certain; but the most extraordinary one is Sir R. Atkins to the famous beauty, Fanny Murray, which I am told either is, or will be soon. I believe I have quite tired you, and will only add my thanks for a very fine guinea-fowl, and beg you will believe me always,

Your affectionate, humble servant.

J. COKE.

Mr. Coke desires his compliments to you and both ours attend Mr. Eyre. I have sent you a pheasant, which was killed yesterday, and if you do not keep it some time it will not be good.

Longford, December the 6th, 1748.

LETTER VI.

With reference to "The Bustles at Derby," Traill, in his Social England, writes: "In nearly all large towns, the assizes, races, or fairs were the occasion of assemblies, balls, card parties, raffling, shops, and plays."

The road between Longford and Derby, even at the present time, is not good, being very much up and down hill, and the distance about ten miles, but when Lady Jane refers to the roads, they were simply tracks through the fields with deep ruts and mud, and there were no bridges over the brooks, which were liable to be flooded, making a journey by carriage disagreeable, and even dangerous. Traill describes the roads in England at this date, and shows how bad they really were : " Highway rates were unknown, and except along the main arteries of communication roads hardly existed. Wheeled carriages were, in country districts, scarcely ever used, the drift lanes, more or less impassable, which communicated between the village and the cultivated lands and ceased when the bounds were reached, could only be called roads by an improbable courtesy."

The reason for the report mentioned in this letter of Lady Townshend's friendship for Lady Huntingdon being extraordinary was, that the former lady had been celebrated for her gallantries and eccentricities. Her maiden name was Etheldreda (or as she preferred to call herself Audrey) Harrison ; she was daughter and sole heiress of Ed. Harrison, Esq., of Balls, Hertfordshire, and was a wit, and was separated from her husband Charles, Viscount Townshend. Walpole calls her " the beautiful Statira," and says " Wit and beauty remain in the persons of Lady Townshend and Lady Caroline Fitzroy " (Petersham). Lady Townshend was the mother of George, first and celebrated Marquis Townshend, and of his still more celebrated brother, the Right Honourable Charles Townshend, orator and statesman.

Jesse records the following specimen of Lady Townshend's wit :—Speaking of the two well known

Sir Thomas Robinsons, of whom the one was tall and thin, the other short and fat, " I can't imagine," she says, " why the one should be preferred to the other ; I see but little difference between them ; the one is as broad as the other is long."

Walpole again says : " Here is another *bon mot* of my Lady Townshend ; we were talking of the Methodists, somebody said 'Pray, Madam, is it true that Whitfield has *re-canted!*' 'No, sir, he has only canted.'"

Lady Townshend died in 1788 and was the supposed original of Lady Bellaston in " Tom Jones," and of Lady Tempest in " Pompey the Little."

Selina Hastings, Countess of Huntingdon, was the second of three daughters and co-heiress of Washington Shirley, second Earl Ferrers. She married the ninth Earl of Huntingdon, and resided with him at Donington Park, Leicestershire. She was known as the Lady Bountiful of her immediate neighbourhood until she turned Methodist. She was very intimate with the two brothers Wesley, and was the first supporter of itinerant preaching, commencing the work by sending her own servant, David Taylor, to preach. The death of her two sons and her husband made her cling more closely to the consolations of religion, and on leaving Donington Park, when her son Francis attained his majority, she took a house at Ashby with her other children and her sisters-in-law, the Ladies Hastings, one of whom married Benjamin Ingham, a zealous disciple of Wesley. Lady Mary Wortley Montagu calls him " a poor wandering Methodist." In 1748 Lady Huntingdon appointed George Whitefield her chaplain, and in order to give him a wider sphere removed to London and opened her house in Park Lane for him to preach in twice a week to the aristocracy. A writer of the period referring to this ardent patroness of Methodism says she may be called "the spiritual spouse of the Rev. S. Wesley."

She made a vain effort to reconcile Whitefield to the Wesleys, and exercised her right as a peeress to appoint as many chaplains as she pleased, and thus protected many clergymen suspected of Methodism.

Walpole writes in 1749, " Methodism is more fashionable than anything but bragg, half the women in the town play very deep at both," and again, " My Lady Huntingdon, the Queen of the Methodists, has got her daughter named Lady of the Bedchamber to the Princesses, but it is all off again, as she will not let her play cards on Sundays."

She remonstrated with the Archbishop of Canterbury (Dr. Cornwallis) for holding routs, and when the remonstrance was fruitless, made her way to Court, and laid her case before George III. and Queen Caroline, by both of whom she was cordially received.

In 1790, she founded an association to perpetuate after her death the religious community over which she exercised morally though not legally entire control. She died the next year, and the connexion named after her still occupies a place amongst religious communities.

Wesley was a great itinerant preacher, and as the churches were shut against him he built spacious meeting houses in London and elsewhere. He quarrelled with Whitefield respecting the doctrine of election, they separated, and the Methodists were denominated according to their respective leaders. Wesley organised and preserved his influence to the last over the society that still continues his name.

The letter, a portion of which is here reproduced,

bearing the autograph of Selina, Countess of Huntingdon, was written to Mr. Cotton of Etwall, Mrs. Eyre's father.

The Rev. Robert Wilmot was Rector of Morley and Mickleover, near Derby, and afterwards appointed a Canon of Windsor. He married, 1746, Dorothy, daughter of Simon Degge, of Derby.

The Fitz-Herberts are a very old Derbyshire family, the present representative being Sir Richard Fitz-Herbert, Bart.,of Tissington, near Ashbourne; a senior branch of the same family also resided in the neighbourhood at Norbury.

The Mrs. Fitz-Herbert here alluded to, we presume to be the wife of Mr. William Fitz-Herbert, of Derby, who died in 1753, "in the flower of her age, distinguished for her piety and fine accomplishments."

The election mentioned in this letter was the contest between Thomas Rivet and Thomas Stanhope as to who should be returned as Member of Parliament for the Borough of Derby in place of the Hon. John Stanhope, deceased, and the result of the poll was a great surprise to many.

The *Gentleman's Magazine* records the fact that the Whigs of Derby resented the candidature of Thomas Stanhope because he had been secretly chosen by a few, and his candidature forced upon them without their cognizance or consent. In order to show their independence they persuaded a fellow-townsman, Thomas Rivet, son of Thomas Rivet, of Derby, to stand in opposition, and with success, for they returned him at the head of the poll.

Horace Walpole writes as follows on the subject :—

"The families of Devonshire and Chesterfield have received a great blow at Derby, where, on the death of John Stanhope, they set up another of the name. Mr.

My Lord desires his Compliments &
I beg mine may be Joyned with Leta & Mrs
Bottom & wish Mr Wilh given whom
I am
your Obliged & faithfull
humble servt S. Huntingdon

Donington Park
apr 26 1742

Rivet, the Duke's chief friend and manager, stood himself and carried it by a majority of seventy-one. Lord Chesterfield had sent down credit for ten thousand pounds."

The *Derby Mercury* of that date says: there was "a great appearance of gentlemen of distinction and fortune, and of great worth and honour." The contest began on Monday morning, and ended on Tuesday evening, and although the crowds were immense the election was carried on in tranquillity and good order.

As a matter of comparison, it may be of interest to mention that the votes polled at this election (December 20th, 1748) were 693, whereas at the last election, in 1895, the number of votes recorded for the return of two members of Parliament were 28,243.

Longford,
December the 30th, 1748.

Dear Madam,

I have often been prevented thanking you for the entertainment your letters gave me, and, to tell the truth, the Bustles at Derby and one's eagerness to hear news, I think, enlivened this part of the world extremely, which at this time of the year wants it, especially with such weather as we have at present; there is no such thing as stirring out for anybody but me, who never catch cold in the country.

Mr. Coke has had a bad cough, but it is now much better. He has desired I would make his compliments to Mr. Eyre and you, and if he shall not be troublesome will wait on you and stay one night when he comes to the sessions at Derby. If I can muster up courage sufficient to venture through the bad roads, it would give me great pleasure to wait on you, but I am such a coward I cannot answer for myself.

All the news I have heard from London, at least the most extraordinary, is Lady Townshend's being much with Lady Huntingdon. Wesley preaches at her house every Thursday and Sunday, and as Lady Huntingdon gives leave to everybody to come who send to desire it, it is now the fashion to go, and Lady Townshend never misses.

We have had Mr. and Mrs. Willmot with us and Mrs. Fitz-Herbert. I think her a very pretty sort of woman. I hope, dear Mrs. Eyre, though the election is over, our correspondence will continue and that you will believe me

Your obliged and affectionate
humble servant,

J. COKE.

My compliments to Mr. Eyre.

LETTER VII.

Lady Jane has been a prisoner in her remote country home, partly through indisposition and the impassability of the roads, but instead of indulging in complaints she patiently and philosophically awaits the time when she will be enabled to visit her friends at Derby. What a contrast this affords to the present time! Imagine a woman of fashion nowadays remaining thus buried alive, for many months entirely cut off from intercourse with her neighbours, and having only very occasional and uncertain communication with the outer world. No daily post, newspapers, or the latest works from the libraries, and the news when it did arrive from London was what would now be considered very stale, being nearly a week old. People in those days were thrown entirely upon their own resources, and yet we hear nothing of boredom and *ennui*.

The Mr. Every mentioned in this letter was High Sheriff of Derbyshire during this year (1749), and at the death of his father became Sir Henry Every, sixth baronet, of Egginton, a place about eight miles from Derby, and a similar distance from Longford.

The death of Miss Kitty Bailey, April 8th, 1752, is thus recorded in " Glover's Derbyshire."

" Last Saturday morning there died Miss Catharine Bailey, daughter of the late Thomas Bailey, Esquire, who was Member of Parliament for the town of Derby 1722—27, and niece to the present Sir Wolstan Dixie, Bart. It is impossible to do this lady's character justice ; she had a form given her above most mortals ; but she never let vanity be the result of it, her chief care was to let it express the noble mind that inhabited this beauteous structure. She had the cardinal virtues united in her ; which with her wisdom and piety enabled her to bear her Creator's pleasure in the abode of trials till she was permitted to receive the reward of the righteous. It may truly be said, though she was very young, she was worthy to be imitated by persons of all ages. All the consolation her acquaintances have is to reflect on her happiness, and to practise her virtues, which will be their gain."

Mr. Rivet *did* remain constant, and married Miss Sibley the next year as an entry in the *Gentleman's Magazine* of that date records his marriage with the "celebrated Miss Sibley." He was Member for Derby 1748—54, and High Sheriff in 1757—63. His younger son was some time Acting Governor of Bombay, and his grandson was created a Baronet as Sir James Rivet-Carnac in 1836, and became Governor of Bombay two years later.

I have been unable to discover why Miss Sibley was celebrated, it may possibly have been for her beauty and wit ; she was the daughter of the Rev. Peter Sibley, of Derby.

Lady Jane here writes of Miss Sibley's exchanging the blue and white cockade for willow-green, and in Letter X. she alludes to a young lady's "wearing the willow," using both expressions as a metaphor to imply mourning for a sweetheart. Fuller says "the willow is a sad tree, whereof such as have lost their love make their mourning garlands." The willow garland was an emblem of being forsaken. "All round my hat I wear a green willow."

Shakespeare says : "I offered him my company to a willow tree . . . . to make him a garland as being forsaken."

The *Gentleman's Magazine* records the acting of the tragedy of *Cato*, on Jan. 4th, 1749, by the children of the Prince and Princess of Wales, with other youths of quality, before a numerous assembly at Leicestershire

House with great applause. It mentions that there had been a rehearsal of the play five days before, and that the prologue was spoken by Prince George, who took the part of Porteous, Prince Edward acted Jaba, and Master Nugent acted Cato. The other masculine characters were: Sempronius, which was taken by Master Evelyn, Lucius by Master Montague, Decius by Lord Milsington, Syphax by Lord North's son, Marcus by Master Madden, Princess Augusta acted Marcia, and the Princess Elizabeth was Lucia. Lady Jane facetiously remarks with regard to the so-called excellence of the acting, "Royal children always excel."

The sudden increase of robbing in the streets was no doubt indirectly due to the peace of Aix-la-Chapelle, and the disbanding of some of the soldiers that had fought in the Austrian war of succession.

Horace Walpole mentions it in 1750 in a letter to Sir Horace Mann. "You will hear little news from England but of robberies; the numbers of disabled soldiers and sailors have all taken to the road, or rather to the street: people are almost afraid of stirring after it is dark. My Lady Albemarle was robbed the other night in Great Russell Street by nine men." "On the preceding day (Jan. 30th), in consequence of persons of distinction who had recently been robbed in the streets, a proclamation appeared in the *London Gazette* offering a reward of one hundred pounds for the apprehension of any robber."

The *Gentleman's Magazine* records that about this time robberies were so frequent in the metropolis that several parishes made voluntary subscriptions for maintaining extraordinary guards for the roads, and published rewards for taking robbers and housebreakers.

The same magazine also refers to the subject in 1751:—"The City of London and its avenues have of late been more than usually infested, not only with a desperate and bloody gang of murderous villains, but with numbers of artful thieves, sharpers, and gamblers, who are daily practising new contrivances to take advantage of the ignorant and unwary."

A rambling writer in the *London Gazetteer* imputes the murders and robberies so frequently among us to the luxury of our superiors, who are the patrons of corruption, and the encouragers of vice and immorality.

The Peak is a district in the northern part of Derbyshire, and Mr. Eyre owned property there.

The ball at Radbourne was one given by the aforementioned German Pole, of Radborne Hall.

Dear Madam,

I was very sorry I could not have the pleasure of waiting on you as I intended, but I never had so bad a cold. You are very good to inquire after me. I am now quite well again, and when the roads and weather are tolerable, will certainly make my first visit to you; but when that will be, is impossible to guess, for at present they are worse than I ever saw them. The two other winters I have stayed at Longford were infinitely better than this, as there is now no possibility of stirring out.

I did not wonder to hear of Mr. Every's being Sheriff. Poor Miss Kitty Bailey is much too handsome to go to London in the way you mention; this is not an age for beauty alone to make their fortune, marrying for Love is quite out of fashion. Will Mr. Rivet remain constant to Miss Sibley in the midst of all the temptations in London? I own I doubt she will exchange the blue and white cockades she wore for his Election for willow-green. I have heard no news worth repeating from London. The Prince of Wales's children acted *Cato* better than anybody ever did; but Royal children, you know, always excel. Everybody writes me word there is such robbing in the streets that it is quite frightful. I believe by all accounts I should be almost as much inclined to stay at home there as here. Mr. Coke desires his compliments to you and Mr. Eyre, and bids me say a great deal to thank you both for the trouble he gave you when he was at Derby. I hope Mr. Eyre is returned safe from the Peak. I beg my compliments, and that you will believe me, very sincerely, dear Madam,

Your affectionate humble servant,

J. COKE.

Longford, January the 20th, 1749.

I hear there has been a ball at Radbourne.

LETTER VIII.

This letter was written in March, 1749. No wonder Lady Jane complains of the distress of the tenants from the cattle plague, which lasted altogether for ten years. It was traced to having been brought from Holland in 1745 by means of two white calves imported by a farmer at Poplar, near London. In September, 1747, mention is made of the suspension of the holding of several large fairs, and it was estimated that 40,000 head of cattle had died in the counties of Derby, Nottingham, and Lincoln. There were constantly recurring outbreaks of the disease during the years 1747, 1748, and 1749; all more or less severe, and amongst them occurred a very bad one in the neighbourhood of Longford in September, 1748, so no doubt during the ensuing six months numbers of the remaining cattle had died, and there would consequently have been much suffering amongst the farmers.

The disease seems to have gone almost unchecked until December, 1749, when there is the record that an order in Council upon the subject was sent to be dispersed in a very expeditious manner by the post-masters. It appears to have been gradually stamped out by legislation during the years 1750, 1751, and 1752, and to have entirely disappeared by 1755.

Numberless remedies and specifics, from wild herbs to hot grog, were constantly prescribed and recorded during these years, and the different reasons given as to the cause of the contagion ranged from the dews and the grass, to the animalculæ of the air.

A great number of butchers were prosecuted for exposing diseased meat for sale during the period of the plague.

Regarding Assemblies, Horace Walpole remarks in a

letter of his, that "Assemblies are now so much in fashion that most persons fancy themselves under a necessity of inviting all their acquaintances three or four times to their houses, not in small parties, which would be supportable, but they are all to come at once; nor is it enough to engage married people; but the boys and girls sit down as gravely at whist-tables as fellows of colleges used to do so formerly. It is actually a ridiculous, though I think a mortifying sight, that play should become the business of the nation, from the age of fifteen to fourscore."

And Lady Mary Wortley-Montagu writes that "Assemblies rage in this part of the world; there is not a street in town free from them, and some spirited ladies go to seven in a night. You need not question but love and play flourish under these encouragements. I now and then peep upon these things with the same coldness I would do on a moving picture; I laugh at some of the motions, wonder at others, and then retire to the elected few that have ears and hear, but mouths have they and speak not."

The Duchess of Bedford was Gertrude, eldest daughter of John, first Earl Gower, and second wife of John, fourth Duke of Bedford, who was Lord Lieutenant in Ireland in 1756. She was noted for her splendour and extravagance.

Traill describes one of her dresses thus: "Her petticoat was green paduasoy, embroidered very richly with gold and silver, and a few colours; the pattern was festoons of shells, corals, corn, cornflowers, and seaweeds."

Lord Fitzwilliam was the third Earl, and married a daughter of the Marquis of Rockingham. He became

Lord of the Bedchamber in 1751, and died aged thirty-seven on August 10th, 1756.

Lady Yarmouth, to whom the dinner was given, was formerly Amelia Sophia de Walmoden, a German lady, and created, in 1739, Baroness and Countess of Yarmouth for life by George II., over whom, Banks in his "Dormant and Extinct Baronage," tells us she possessed great influence, and was able to dispense to her favourites places, pensions, and honours. As we find Lord Fitzwilliam within two years appointed to a high position at Court, it may be that he was ingratiating himself into the good graces of this influential lady by giving a costly entertainment, a method not yet gone out of fashion.

The Princess here alluded to was the Princess of Wales, who on March 19th, 1749, was safely delivered of a daughter.

Longford,
Tuesday morn.

Indeed I must own, dear Mrs. Eyre, that of all the time I ever passed in Derbyshire this winter has been the most melancholy, and I don't find it mends, for the continual rains have made the roads worse than ever I knew them. I flattered myself that sometime towards the middle of this month I might wait on you, but 'tis impossible this terrible weather, and the distress of the tenants from the distemper among the cattle makes the country at present not the most cheerful habitation. London is as gay as ever, and insensible of all these misfortunes. Assemblies abound, the Duchess of Bedford has a general one every Friday during Lent, but nothing has made so great a noise as a supper Lord Fitzwilliam gave to Lady Yarmouth. The company consisted of twenty people, and there was ninety-two dishes, besides a magnificent dessert. Those of the Prince's Court are greatly alarmed for the Princess, her reckoning is out. I shall really be very glad to hear of her being safe in bed.

I hope you will continue well. I was some time ago very much out of order, but am now recovered. Mr. Coke desires his compliments to you, we both beg ours to Mr. Eyre, and that you will believe me, dear madam,

Your most affectionate humble servant,

J. COKE.

LETTER IX.

This letter is written from the Cokes' house in London.

Many people of note resided in Savile Row, Burlington Gardens. It was so called after the heiress of the Saviles, Dorothy, daughter and heir of the celebrated George Savile, Marquis of Halifax, and wife of Richard Boyle, Earl of Burlington, the amateur architect.

Scarcely has Lady Jane arrived in town or recovered from the fatigue of the journey, after a year and a half's seclusion in the country, although still feeling unfit for the general bustles, she has nevertheless twice indulged in the game of Bragg.

A verse on Bragg from the "Modern Fine Lady" tersely exemplifies the craze.

> " Breakfasts and auctions wear the morn away,
> Each evening gives an opera or a play;
> Then Brag's eternal joys all night remain,
> And kindly usher in the morn again."

Bragg was a game of cards played by any number of persons; the dealer giving three cards to each person at one time, and turning up the last card all round. This being done, each player puts down three stakes, one for each card. The first stake is won by the best card turned up in the deal, beginning with the ace and so on. When cards of the same value are turned up to two or more, the eldest hand gains; but the ace of diamonds wins to whatever hand it be turned up.

The second stake is won by what is called the bragg, which consists in one of the players challenging the rest to turn up cards equal to his. A pair of aces is the best bragg, and pair of kings the next, and so on; and a pair of any sort wins the stake from the most valuable single card. In this consists the great diversion of the game, for by plausible management a pair of fives, trois, or even deuces, in the hands of a clever player, may outbragg a much higher pair, and even some pairs royal. The knave of clubs is here a principal favourite, making a pair with any other card in hand, and with any other two cards a pair royal.

The third stake is won by the person who first makes up the cards in his hand to one and thirty; each court card going for ten, and drawing from the pack, as usual in this game.

Lady Mary Wortley-Montagu writes: "Your new-fashioned game of brag was the genteel amusement when I was a girl, crimp succeeded to that and basset, and hazard employed the town when I left it to go to Constantinople. At my return I found them all at commerce, which gave place to quadrille, and that to whist; but the rage of play has been ever the same, and will ever be so among the idle of both sexes."

A punning rhymster of the period thus writes of Bragg, and the verses seem sufficiently amusing and illustrative of the times to reproduce:—

> Ye belles and ye beaux for a moment attend,
> And give ear to the wholesome advice of a friend;
> Haste, haste altogether, not one of you lag,
> Whilst I sing of that noble diversion called Bragg.
>   Sing tantara ra ra Bragg all.
>
> Some over-nice criticks indeed may cry shame,
> And tell you 'tis wicked and sinful to game,
> But I'll show you from beginning of life to its fag
> We all are at play, and the world is a Bragg.
>   Sing tantara ra, &c.
>
> The statesman braggs high and makes every place ring,
> So we're sure he must bragg on no less than a king;
> But if any one *sees* him, his boasting he'll leave,
> For he built all his hopes on the head of a knave.
>   Sing tantara ra, &c.
>
> The Church, like the State, braggs of wisdom and merit,
> How he conquers the flesh by the strength of the spirit,
> But as soon as his rev'rence is under the pall,
> 'Tis confessed that he bragg'd upon nothing at all.
>   Sing tantara ra, &c.
>
> The soldier boasts much of his courage and might,
> How many he has killed, and how daring in fight,
> But if challeng'd, the hero the interview wards,
> And rather than venture he throws up the cards.
>   Sing tantara ra, &c.

Sage physick, that makes such a show with his skill,
If you live 'tis his work, if you die 'tis God's will,
Makes a boast that he keeps us in health—a queer wag,
And so cheats us out of our lives by a Bragg.
    Sing tantara ra, &c.

The lawyer too braggs of his conscience and worth;
Believe him, there's not such a man upon earth;
But you'll find if you look in his worship's green bag,
That he, like the rest, has been playing at Bragg.
    Sing tantara ra, &c.

If the women lose all, and have nothing to pay,
The men they must satisfy in the old way;
Like the men (for their cases are not a whit worse),
They give 'em their honour in lieu of their purse.
    Sing tantara ra, &c.

Her Ladyship braggs on her high education;
She has gleaned both the *French* and the *English* nation,
But when once got to cards her politeness will lag,
And my lady you find a virago at *Bragg*.
    Sing tantara ra, &c.

The commoner's wife braggs of her, and her spouse,
She at cards makes a noise, he a noise in the house;
And if she be a gamester, pray tell me, sirs, who
Can swear that she is not a *commoner* too?
    Sing tantara ra, &c.

Chloe cheats ev'ry beau with as easy an air
As if quite unconscious of playing unfair;
They wisely consider, so ne'er make a pother,
If she cheats at one game, she'll play fair at another.
    Sing tantara ra, &c.

Thus moralists preach, but ne'er heed what they say,
Nor for their odd fancies desist from your play;
But whilst you have character, money, or rag,
Ne'er throw up the cards till you've lost them at *Bragg*.
    Sing tantara ra, &c.

The *Gentleman's Magazine* records that "on November 19th, 1749, the birthday of H. R. H. the Princess of Wales who then entered the thirty-first year of her age,

His Majesty received the compliments of the nobility and gentry, when there was the most splendid Court on that occasion ever known." So no doubt the preparations must have been commenced some while beforehand, and the forthcoming reception was evidently much discussed.

The Lady Seymours, who were great heiresses, were Lady Frances and Lady Charlotte Seymour, daughters of the sixth Duke of Somerset, by his second marriage with the Lady Charlotte Finch, daughter of the Earl of Winchelsea. The Duke, who died Dec. 2nd, 1748, bequeathed to them both very large fortunes. Lady Frances married the Marquis of Granby, son of the third and father of the fourth Duke of Rutland, on Sept. 3rd, 1750, and Lady Charlotte married the third Earl of Aylesford, Oct. 6th, 1750.

The French Ambassadress was Madame de Mirepoix, the second wife of that brave soldier the Marquis de Mirepoix, Marshal of France, and Ambassador to England, who was made a Duke in 1751, and Horace Walpole says he "was much esteemed in England, having little of the manners of his country."

His wife was a woman of ability, and was long in great favour with Louis XV. and his successive mistresses, and particularly with Madame du Barri, whose cause she espoused, doing herself no good thereby, and also quarrelling with her family. She was the daughter of Prince Craon, a noble of Anjou.

Horace Walpole writes in 1748 with reference to Madame de Mirepoix, "I like her extremely, though she likes nothing but gaming," and in 1750, "At a ball Lord Sandwich gave, Madame de Mirepoix and the Duchess of Bedford were the rival queens. Their host *contrived* to be on the outside of the door to hand down to supper whatever lady came out first; the latter made a feint offer to the Ambassadress to go first, she returned it, and the other briskly accepted it, upon which the Ambassadress with great cleverness made all the other women go before her, and then asked the Duke of Bedford if he would go, too. However, though they continue to visit, the wound is incurable; you don't imagine that a widow of the House of Lorraine and a daughter of Princess Craon can digest such an affront. It certainly was very absurd, as she is not only an Ambassadress but a stranger, and consequently all English women, as being at home, should give her place."

The French Ambassadress was a leader of fashion, and one of the principal ladies in society during her husband's term ôf appointment.

The *Gentleman's Magazine* records the fact that "On July 22nd, 1755, the Duc de Mirepoix, the French Ambassador, set out for the Court of France; his Excellency having notice given him from the Lords of the Regency to depart this kingdom as soon as possible."

"Our Dancing Friend" is Mrs. Barnes, alluded to in Letter V.

As has already been mentioned in the introduction to Letter II., " Madame Sal:" was Hester Salusbury Cotton, and lived with the Eyres in Derby. Mrs. Eyre, having no children of her own, seems almost to have adopted her young niece, a daughter, and the youngest of the ten children of Sir Lynch Salusbury Cotton. I hope that now this little girl, so often alluded to, will take some tangible form in the reader's imagination, and therefore I reproduce a letter written by her about this

Derby June 17th 1749

Dear Sir

I have sent you the Song with a new wau. of saying up a letter which would trouany secure, it for Bells, Mr Order my writing Master taught me; They my Duty to my Grand Mama and my love to Aunt Kitty

& I am Dear Sir your Most Dutyfull and affectionate Grand daughter Salusbury Cotton

time, and addressed to her grandfather, Rowland Cotton, of Etwall, but omitting the song referred to, which was a rollicking one sung by Mr. Beard at Ranelagh, and of no interest to us now. The letter was evidently Madam Sal:'s unaided composition, as the spelling is amusingly phonetic, and is an interesting example of a child's writing, and of the dutiful expressions usual at that period.

The "Grandma" alluded to was Mary, or as she preferred to call herself, "Stella," daughter and co-heiress of Sir Samuel Sleigh, of Ashe, the wife of Rowland Cotton, and the mother of Mrs. Eyre.

"Aunt Kitty" married Robert Shirley, afterwards sixth Earl Ferrers. Her eldest son, Robert, seventh Earl, had an only son, who married Caroline, only daughter of the second Lord Scarsdale, and predeceased his father, leaving no issue, and the present representative of the title is a descendant of her second son, Washington Shirley, eighth Earl Ferrers.

Madam Sal: was evidently quite a scribe, for in Letter XII. Lady Jane sends her a present of some French paper, "as she knows she likes writing," and elsewhere alludes to her as being "so good a correspondent."

In March, 1759, Hester Salusbury (Madam Sal:) was still living with the Eyres, for Elizabeth Cotton, her sister, afterwards married to Colonel D'Avenant, writing from London, gives the following messages : "I am much obliged to sister Sal: for the nosegay, Mama sends blessing to sister Sal:, pray my love." She married Sir Corbet Corbet, who was a son of Thomas D'Avenant, of Clearbrook, Herts, by Anne, his wife, daughter and heir of Sir Roger Corbet, of Stoke, and took his maternal patronymic ; he was created a Baronet in 1786, and died without issue in 1823, thus surviving his wife, who died in 1822, by one year, and as there was no issue the title became extinct. He devised his Adderley estates to his nephew, Richard Corbet, Esq., second son of Sir Andrew Corbet, Bart., in whose family they still remain, and his other property he left to the Cotton family.

The family at Etwall were of course the Cottons.

Saville Row,
November the 1st, 1749.

As I ordered the groom to call on dear Mrs. Eyre, in his return from hence, I need not now tell you any particulars of our journey, the fatigue of which I have but just recovered. A year-and-half's quiet in the country, I find, makes one rather unfit for the bustles of London, which I have had yet very little share in, tho' I have twice played at Bragg, which seems to be the great business of everybody here. The Birthday, and the Lady Seymours, are at present the subjects of conversation. The French Ambassadress and the Duchess of Bedford were the two finest women; the first is the pattern for dress, she is not young, but seems to forget that as much as our Dancing Friend; her hair is curled in small ringlets round her face, pinned up behind, a cap not near so big as your hand, and nothing about her neck; 'tis the business of all the great people to entertain her, and she never dines without four courses, and sitting near four hours at dinner; but I forget that this is to be a letter of business. Enclosed you will find the draught of what your cross may be; if you please to bestow ten guineas then it would be very handsome, but five would do nothing, the cheapest way it can be done would come to between eight and nine pounds. I would not let the solitaire be unset till I had your directions. The shell-pearl drops for Miss Cotton's ear-rings will be 30s., and a cross the same. I can't yet meet with what I like, when I do she shall know the price. I beg you will make my best compliments to Mr. Eyre and Madam Sal:, and believe me, dear Mrs. Eyre,

Your most affectionate humble servant,

J. COKE.

Mr. Coke desires his compliments, and we shall be obliged to you to make both ours to the family at Etwall.

LETTER X.

In this letter, written in January, 1750, Lady Jane is already looking forward to the pleasure of seeing her Derbyshire friends the following May, little dreaming of the trouble and loss that were in store for her in the death of her husband, and that she never again would reside at Longford and be the queen of county society.

Mrs. Cibber, the actress, was Susannah Maria,

daughter of Mr. Arne, an upholsterer of Covent Garden. She was sister to the composer Arne, and married, against her will, a widower called Theophilus Cibber, an ugly man of small stature, and of extravagant and vicious habits. She had a fine voice of great sweetness, if not of remarkable power, and in December, 1741, sang *The Messiah* so well that Dr. Delany, the friend and companion of Dean Swift, made the following remark: " Woman, for this all thy sins are forgiven thee." Her reputation as a singer soon became merged in that of a great tragic actress; in a few years she attained to great eminence.

As Constance, in *King John*, Mrs. Cibber surpassed all that have followed her, also as Ophelia. Three years after the date of this letter, in 1753, she joined Garrick at Drury Lane, and as a tragic actress more than excelled, but failed in comedy. When Garrick heard of her death on the 30th of January, 1766, he exclaimed, " Then tragedy is dead on one side." She was interred in one of the cloisters belonging to Westminster Abbey.

"The Little Theatre in the Haymarket" was so called to distinguish it from the larger King's Theatre, which was also in the Haymarket.

French players had been no uncommon spectacle in England, and the foundation of the animosity against them was as follows. The opposition to the Court had proceeded so far as to be on the point of ridiculing the King publicly on the stage of the Little Theatre in the Haymarket. Sir R. Walpole, having intelligence of this design, frustrated it, and procured the passing of an Act in 1737 for regulating the stage, by which all plays, &c., had to be subjected to the Lord Chamberlain. This provoked the people so much that, this French company having obtained a licence at a time when several English companies were cashiered, it was made a party point to silence foreigners ; and when these French players appeared the audience and populace would not suffer them to perform. Several young men of quality drew their swords in the riot, endeavouring to support them, and Lord Trentham's being present was exaggerated into his being their chief protector.

Lord Trentham was the eldest son of the first Earl Gower, whom he succeeded in 1754, being afterwards created Marquis of Stafford. He died in 1803, and his son was made Duke of Sutherland in 1833. Viscount Trentham was returned to Parliament unopposed for the city of Westminster in 1747, but had to vacate his seat upon being appointed one of the Lords of the Admiralty, and seek re-election, but this time, although he ultimately retained his seat, the contest was a severe one, owing to his actions with regard to the French players.

The election and the scrutiny are thus referred to by Horace Walpole in 1749. " The mob was determined not to suffer French players, and Lord Trentham's engaging in their defence was made great use of against him at the ensuing election for Westminster, where he was to be re-chosen on being appointed a Lord of the Admiralty."

" All our conversation has turned on the Westminster election, on which, after a vast struggle, Lord Trentham had the majority."

" Then came the scrutiny. After a week's squabbling on the right of election, the High Bailiff declared what he would take to be the right. They are now proceeding to disqualify votes on that foot, but as his decision could not possibly please both sides, I fear it will come to us at last."

And again on January 31st, 1750, a little later than the date of this letter, Horace Walpole writes :

"The Westminster election is still hanging in scrutiny; the Duke of Bedford paid the election, which he owns to have cost seven thousand pounds ; and my Lord Gower pays the scrutiny, which will be at least as much."

"An Act for the more effectual preventing excessive and deceitful gaming" gave notice that after June 24th, 1745, no person shall keep a house or place for playing roly-poly (a certain pernicious game called roulet) or other game with cards or dice, otherwise there was but little restriction on gambling until 1752, when it was put down by an Act of that year which provided for the licensing of all houses of entertainment and music halls, and made it penal to allow gambling or disorderly behaviour in them.

Blowzabella was the nickname given to Mrs. Barnes, no doubt on account of her ungainly and untidy appearance.

Presumably an inferior company of actors had paid Derby a visit, and Mrs. Eyre had found fault with their acting. Glover says "There was formerly no regular theatre in Derby, and itinerant performers occasionally exhibited dramatic pieces in private rooms or in the barns of inns."

Hutton, in his history of Derby, says "The exhibitions on the stage were held in a boothe in Iron Gate till 1773."

Mr. John Fitz-Herbert was Vicar of Ashbourne, and the *Derby Mercury* of June 7th, 1751, mentions that he was to preach at Derby.

Mr. Meynell was Godfrey of Meynell Langley, and of the same family as the Meynells of Bradley. Horace Walpole relates an amusing story of one of these Meynells, and describes him "as a big hunting man, who, when engaged to dine at a formal old lady's, he stayed so late out hunting that he had no time to dress but went as he was with many apologies."

The well-known Meynell hounds, now a subscription pack, formerly belonged to this family, whose name they still bear.

Hutton relates an amusing story illustrative of the economy practised even in large houses, and mentions that while the Meynell family were spending their sober evening by the glow of their own fire, a coach and six was heard rolling up to the door. "Bring candles," says the lady of the mansion with some emotion, while she stepped forward to receive the guests; but instantly returning, "Light up a rush," said she, "'tis only my cousin Curzon."

Kitty Bailey has already been alluded to in the introductory remarks of Letter VII.

I have twice been confined with violent colds, and really not able to write, or I should sooner have returned, dear Mrs. Eyre, my thanks for the pleasure your letter gave me. Whatever amusements I meet with here, I assure you, do not make me forget my Derbyshire friends, and I often think with great pleasure on the month of May, when I hope we shall all meet, well and in good spirits, and the Queen begin again to give laws to her subjects, who she apprehends may forget their obedience in so long an absence; pray tell them so. London will very soon be quite full. I know very little of the publick spectacles. Mrs.

Cibber not being on the stage is a great hurt in my opinion to the plays. Operas there are none but at the Little Theatre in the Haymarket, and I hear so bad a character of them that I do not think them worth risking a cold to go to. I conclude you heard a great deal about the French players; they are gone, as I believe nobody would have courage enough to have appeared in their favour. Lord Trentham has suffered extremely for subscribing to them. The Election was a vast expense, and the Scrutiny will be still more; but money is only scarce with people in the country, here is no appearance of the want of it. Play is really grown to such an excess that it is amazing, among the women as well as men; everything is much dearer than I ever knew, particularly silks. I had wrote so far when I received the pleasure of your letter. I think myself very much obliged to you for it, and telling me so much news. Believe me, dear Mrs. Eyre, nobody wishes you and Mr. Eyre, not forgetting Madam Sal:, more Happy New Years than I do. I'm glad Derby has been so gay this winter. Bad actors are better than none. The Assemblies I doubt will never prosper whilst Blowzabella presides. I am surprised to hear all Mr. John Fitz-Herbert's low spirits end in matrimony, tho' I think it extremely in fashion in Derbyshire, and wish our friend Mr. Meynell would follow so many good examples. Poor Kitty Bailey has been so long a beauty that I doubt she will wear the willow, and not succeed with your clergyman. You are very good to enquire so much about my health. The country certainly agrees with me, for there I never catch cold, and here I am never without one. However, I am now pretty well. You say nothing of your cross. Pray tell me if I should send your solitaire and Miss Cotton's ear-rings. I should be afraid to venture them by the waggon, but will follow any directions you give, and if you have anything to do here, I beg you will employ me. As for fashions, according to the English custom we follow the French Ambassadress. Very few night-gowns, or gowns and petticoats, but at Court; various sorts of caps, but chiefly made of blonde, as well as ruffles and tippets. Mr. Coke joins in compliments to Mr. Eyre, and his Flirt, Madam Sal:, and I am, in great truth,

   Your affectionate and obliged
      humble servant,
         J. COKE.

Saville Row, January the 2nd, 1750.

 My best wishes always attend the family at Etwall.

LETTER XI.

Lady Jane evidently executed a great many commissions and did a good deal of shopping for Mrs. Eyre.

Traill, in his "Social England," says:—"All ladies who had London friends did their shopping by letter, and all dress materials, even lawn for babies' night-caps, were sent from town."

There is something pathetic in this letter, for in it Lady Jane describes her husband's health, and excuses herself from giving any news as her time has been occupied in attending to him; she adds, however, that he is getting better and all danger past, and that they are going out together to take the air; all this shows that Lady Jane little imagined that before the day was ended Mr. Coke would have died, and she would be a widow for the second time.

I do think I had some reason to complain of dear Mrs. Eyre for her long silence; tho' I allow Derby a very genteel place, yet I may venture to say you have not quite so many engagements as your London correspondents. I beg you will leave off calling any commission you give me, either from yourself or Etwall, by the name of trouble, since I assure you very sincerely I shall never think it so. I have ventured to buy Miss Cotton a pair of Scots-pebble ear-rings and cross, with another pair of drops for her diamond tops. I met with them very cheap, for the whole purchase is but two guineas and a half; they are extremely the fashion and in my opinion very pretty. Your solitaire remains as it was, since it is better not to alter it, unless it was made more expensive than you seem at present to care for. I shall deliver all these things to whoever comes with a note from either you or Miss Cotton.

I am sure you will be sorry to have so bad an account as I have to give of Mr. Coke's health. He has had a hoarseness and cough all the winter, but his cough has increased so much that he is attended by a physician, and has not been out in an evening this fortnight. It comes by fits with a shortness of breath; the learned says it does not affect his lungs, but is a gouty humour; he looks much better than you would imagine, sleeps well, and I think I may assure you he is better to-day than he has been for some time, so that I hope the worst is over. I am going out with him this morning to take the air, which he is ordered to do constantly, therefore you will excuse my telling you no news, and only adding our compliments to your family both at Derby and Etwall, and assuring dear Mrs. Eyre that I am with great truth her

   Sincere and faithful humble servant,
          J. COKE.

Saville Row, February the 26th, 1750.
I think the velvet will do extremely well.

LETTER XII.

No doubt some intervening letters are missing here, and it is regretable that there is a gap of seven months between this letter and the last. The widowed Lady Jane in the meanwhile has been to Tunbridge Wells to take the waters there, and has just returned again to her London house, and is suggesting plans to revisit Derby, and to stay with the Eyres.

Lady Jane complains of not daring to hold down her head after taking the waters; possibly this was done so as not to retard their proper digestion, and to prevent giddiness, for a treatise of the middle of the last century on drinking these waters says: "Where the constitution is too delicate, and the nervous system too exquisitely sensible, surprising as it may appear to those who are unacquainted with these waters, each single dose will sometimes produce a giddiness, especially at the beginning of the course."

Lady Jane was very pleased to leave Tunbridge Wells, and did not enjoy her stay there at all, for as she was all the time in deep mourning, she could not join in the gaieties or social life of the place, which are somewhat quaintly described in "Topographical Tracts," wherein a delightful review of life at Tunbridge Wells at this period is given. "People of the greatest title, rank, and dignity, people of every learned profession, of every religious and political persuasion; people of every degree, condition, and occupation of life (if well dressed and well behaved), meet amicably here together; some for the benefit of the water and air, some for a little relaxation from study and business, and others for the pleasures of social and polished life.

"And really, the appearance of the company when assembled together is quite beautiful and noble in the daytime, moving along the parade, like a walking parterre, and at night, in the rooms, like a galaxy of stars in a bright nocturnal sky. The morning is passed in an undress; in drinking the waters, in private and public breakfastings, which are sometimes given by one of the company, in attending prayers at the chapel, in social converse on the parade, at the coffee-house, in the public rooms, or booksellers' shops; billiards, cotillon dances, private concerts, cards, or sometimes adventitious and extraordinary curiosity and novelty; a painter, a musician, a juggler, a fire-eater, or a philosopher, &c.

"After dinner all go dressed to the parade again, and the rooms, to tea, in private parties or in public. The ball nights are Tuesdays and Fridays, and assemblies and cards every other night except Sundays.

"While the company are walking on the parade, a band of music plays to them from the orchestra twice in the morning, before and after prayers, and once again in the evening, unless it be a ball night.

"A few minutes are spent by some in making verses, as the waters, or genius of the place, or as love and leisure inspire. These verses *(jeux d' esprits)* are various and occasional, but chiefly complimentary to the ladies in general, or to some particular fair one. A copy of them is usually left at the bookseller's shop, and entered in a book there for inspection and entertainment of the company. This poetical pastime, when confined within the bounds of decorum and politeness, is very pleasing and agreeable, and is always supposed to be exempt of criticism.

"Mr. Addison, in the *Guardian*, remarks that 'the

water poets are an innocent tribe, and deserve all the encouragment I can give them. It would be barbarous to treat these authors with bitterness, who never write out of season, and whose words are useful with the waters.'

"These are the amusements which are chiefly confined to the walks. The outward amusements are cricketing, horse races, and other diversions; such as walking, riding, and airing in carriages on the contiguous heaths and commons, or excursions to some of the most remarkable places in the environs of the Wells."

It is not unlikely that this Miss Roach mentioned was one of the four daughters of Mr. Edward Roach, of Trabolgan, County Cork, as some of his children died in France. He was the ancestor of the present Lord Fermoy.

Lord Vane was William, second Viscount Vane. His wife, nicknamed "Lady Frail," was the too celebrated Lady Vane, first married clandestinely to Lord William Hamilton, and secondly to Lord Vane. She has given her extraordinary and disreputable adventures to the world in Smollett's novel "Peregrine Pickle," under the title of "Memoirs of a Lady of Quality." She was the daughter of Mr. Hawes, a South Sea director, and died in 1788, a year before her husband.

Horace Walpole says, "My Lady Vane has literally published the memoirs of her own life. Her adventures are worthy to be bound up with those of my good sister-in-law (Lady Walpole); the German Princess, an impostor of Charles II.'s time; and Moll Flanders."

Sir Walter Scott says, "She not only furnished Smollett with the materials for recording her own infamy, but rewarded him handsomely for the insertion of her story."

The publication of her memoirs brought forth a letter animadverting upon her own conduct, and showing that the behaviour of her husband gave no reasons for it, and describing how she cajoles him, and almost ruins him by her constant requests for money; at the same time the writer owns that Lord Vane is weak and foolish as far as she is concerned, but that was no excuse for the profligacy and unchastity of her behaviour. Lord Vane, having obtained sufficient proofs, commenced divorce proceedings, but she flattered him so that he withdrew his libel, and she saved by that means fifteen hundred a year jointure.

Lady Mary Wortley-Montagu says in a letter to Lady Pomfret: "I am told, though she (Lady Vane) does not pique herself upon fidelity of any one man (which is but a narrow way of thinking), she boasts that she has always been true to her nation, and notwithstanding foreign attacks, has always reserved her charms for the use of her own countrymen."

Horace Walpole writes in one of his letters as follows:—"You cannot imagine what an entertaining fourth act of the opera we had the other night. Lord Vane in the middle of the pit making love to my lady. The Duke of Newcastle has lately given him three score thousand pounds to consent to cut off the entail of the Newcastle Estate. The fool immediately wrote to his wife to beg she would return to him from Lord Berkeley (Augustus, fourth Earl of Berkeley), that he had got so much money, and now they might live comfortably; but she will not live comfortably, she is at Lord Berkeley's house, whither go divers after her."

It is recorded that on one occasion she asked forty

ladies to a public breakfast at Tunbridge Wells, and was not favoured with the company of one of them.

Both correspondents evidently had no liking for Mrs. Barnes, "the lady of the Derby Assembly," for she is constantly called "Blowzabella," and disparaging remarks are made about her.

The following is taken from Glover's "History of Derby," anent the Derby races:—"Derby races on Sinfen Moor, on August 6th, 1748, for three subscription purses of £50 each, at which there was a great meeting of gentlemen and others each day, and the diversions gave great satisfaction to the spectators, being conducted with great regularity and order. It appears to have been customary at this time for the horses to run three heats, notwithstanding the first two were won by one horse. This was the case in each of the three days at the races." And again later he remarks, " At the races on Sinfen Moor there was the greatest number of the nobility and gentry of the first rank ever known."

Sinfen Moor was a large unenclosed common of 894 acres in extent.

Lady Jane playfully calls Mr. Eyre "her subject," designating his house "her palace," and herself as his queen, and she has once more commenced to look forward to a visit to Derby the following summer to see her many friends in the neighbourhood. This autumn Lady Jane has evidently arranged to go elsewhere, for she mentions a round of three visits to intimate friends or connections, all within a few miles of one another. The Finchs and Rockinghams were all related by marriage to the Cokes.

The first visit was to Mr. Finch, who was the Honourable Edward Finch, fifth son of the sixth Earl of

Winchelsea, and married to the daughter and co-heiress of Sir Thomas Palmer, Bart., of Wingham, Kent. Mr. Finch had been employed as a diplomat, and became subsequently one of the Grooms of the Bedchamber, and Master of the Robes. He was Member of Parliament for the University of Cambridge, and took the name of Hatton in 1764 in consequence of inheriting the fortune of his maternal uncle, Viscount Hatton. He died in 1771. His daughter Anne was a god-child of Lady Jane, who generously remembered her, and left her the sum of five hundred guineas in her will.

Lord Winchelsea was Daniel, seventh Earl, whose second spouse was a sister of his brother Edward's wife, and was the other daughter and co-heiress of Sir Thomas Palmer.

Horace Walpole, in one of his letters, remarks, "Ned Finch is made Groom of the Bedchamber, which was vacant, and Will Finch Vice-chamberlain, which was not vacant," and also records that these three celebrated brothers were called by Sir Charles Hanbury Williams on account of the darkness of their complexion, "the dark or black funereal Finches."

William Finch's place was Kirby Hall, in Northamptonshire, and is described in the "Beauties of England and Wales" as a fine mansion dating from 1590. It contained a fine collection of paintings and sculptures, and was considered one of the best furnished houses of the kingdom. The gardens were adorned with numerous exotic and indigenous plants, and the wilderness in the park contained almost every variety of English tree.

Lady Jane's next visit was to Lord Winchelsea, at Burley House, in Rutlandshire, on the borders of

Northamptonshire, of which place there is an engraving in the "Beauties of England and Wales," and it is described as being situated on a hill, which rises abruptly from the vale of Catmose. " It was so strong a place that the Parliamentarians, being unable to defend such an extensive line of defence, burnt it down, so that it should not fall into the hands of the Royalist party. It was many years after the Restoration before the house was rebuilt by the Earl of Nottingham, who enclosed the park with a stone wall of nearly six miles round. The style of architecture is of the Doric order, but not overloaded with ornament. The house is superbly and elegantly furnished, but even the best apartments are not too magnificent to be comfortable, and numerous portraits and paintings adorn the walls. The views of the house from different parts of the garden are very striking, and the gardens themselves have some of the ancient regularity of alleys, lawns, and parterres. A lovely view looking down upon the gardens is obtained from the roof of the house, and from it the visitor may see the whole of the diminutive county of Rutland."

Lady Jane's third visit was to her friend Lady Rockingham, who was formerly Lady Mary Finch, a sister of the afore-mentioned Earl of Winchelsea. She had married the Earl of Malton, K.G., afterwards created Marquis of Rockingham, and had a son and daughter. At the death of the former the title became extinct, and the latter married the third Earl Fitzwilliam, of whom the present holder of the title is a direct descendant.

Lady Rockingham lived at Rockingham, which the "Beauties of England and Wales" describes as "a spacious and fine old house, built within the court of Rockingham Castle, and amidst the ruins of what once had been a strong fortress, situated on the top of a hill in the Rockingham forest." William the Conqueror is said to have commenced the castle, which became an occasional residence of our early kings. More than twenty despatches in the eighth year of Edward the Third bear date at this place, which is also celebrated for the council of nobility, bishops, and clergy who sat here in 1094, for the purpose of terminating the dispute between William Rufus and Anselm, Archbishop of Canterbury, respecting the right investiture and obedience to the see of Rome. This castle was strongly fortified with double embattled walls, numerous towers, and other bulwarks, and further secured by a large and strong keep. In the time of Leland, who describes it, many of the works were standing, but in a very decayed state, and little of the original building now remains except its grand entrance-arched-gateway, flanked by two massive bastion towers.

Sir Edward Watson, father of the first Baron Rockingham, had the following apothegm written in letters of gold on the beams of the castle hall :—

THE : HOWSE : SHAL : BE : PRESERVED
AND : NEVER : WIL : DECAYE
WHEARE : THE : ALMIGHTY : GOD : IS : HONORED
AND : SERVED : DAYE : BY : DAYE 1579.

Mrs. Egerton lived at Foston, in Derbyshire, and had formerly been one of Lady Jane's county neighbours.

I would not begin a letter to you from Tunbridge, my dear Mrs. Eyre, as holding down my head with the waters was very disagreeable to me. They have done me a great deal of good, but I was never better pleased with leaving any place, for it is only amusing to those who pass their time in public. I who never went in to the rooms grew extremely tired. There was a great deal of company, and some beauties, but by all I heard the men's attachment was to the gaming-tables, and not to the ladies. A Miss Roach, educated in France, was the most admired. She is entirely French, so much so in her behaviour that such an awkward Englishwoman as myself would think her rather odd than pleasing. Lady Vane was there with her lord, and began several balls. She seems quite easy, though no woman of any rank took the least notice of her. In my whole life I never saw anybody altered to the degree she is. I have not seen her near since her days of innocence and beauty, and really should not have known her if I had not been told her name, as there is not the least remains of what she was. If anybody has a mind to learn new fashions, I would advise their going to Tunbridge, where they abound, and I don't think even Blowzabella in her flounces came up to some figures I saw in a morning, and I was told that at the balls they outdid their usual outdoings. Skeleton caps without number (which I conclude you have seen), made of colours, but I suppose at your Races you saw a great variety, and hope you were well diverted at them, and shall be very glad to have some accounts from you of your amusements. Remember how long you were before you gave me the pleasure of answering my last letter, and don't be so lazy for the future. Be assured I am always extremely glad to hear from you, and could not have greater pleasure than to see you and a few more of my Derbyshire neighbours. I hope next summer, if you will be troubled with me, and my subject continues to remember his queen enough to give her leave to visit her palace in Derby, I shall be very happy to come to you, and make my visits from your house. It is a great while to come, but I please myself with thinking on this scheme, if it does not prove disagreeable to you or Mr. Eyre. I beg my best compliments to him, and Madam Sal:, as I know she loves writing, I have sent her enclosed some French paper. The weather is now much too fine for London, yet I am here, wishing myself extremely in the country. I arrived but last Saturday from Tunbridge, and propose staying but a few days longer. I am got into my new house, and vastly busy in hanging pictures, &c. When all is done that I intend it will be very neat and comfortable, which is all not only that I pretend to, but wish for, since I have long known magnificence never made happiness. I beg my best compliments to the family at Etwall, and am very glad Mrs. Cotton liked her tippet; if she or any of you have any commands here, I shall take it very ill if anybody else is employed. I go hence to Mr. Finch's and Lord Winchelsea's, which are not much out of my way to Lady Rockingham's, where I shall stay till the latter end of the next month or the beginning of October, then return hither and settle for the winter. London is quite deserted, therefore I can tell you no sort of news from hence. Pray let me hear from you very soon, and believe me, dear Mrs. Eyre,

Yours most sincerely,

J. COKE.

Saville Row, August the 21st, 1750.

When you see Mrs. Egerton be so good to make my compliments.

LETTER XIII.

An interval of some months has elapsed since the former letter, and Lady Jane has had little spare time for writing, having been much occupied since Mr. Coke's death with business matters, and in changing her house, having moved to another, and probably a smaller, house in Saville Row, and in spite of having so short a distance to transfer her possessions, she seems to find it a more troublesome business than she anticipated. She, however, found it possible to pay some visits in the country, and in particular to Lady Rockingham in Northamptonshire.

"As absolute as the King of France" was an expression of the period, as Louis XV. ruled his kingdom in a most autocratic manner. This belief in the power and security of French monarchs was afterwards rudely dispelled by the events which culminated in the horrors of the French Revolution, and the beheading of Louis XVI. and Marie Antoinette.

Sir Nathaniel Curzon of Kedleston, was Member of Parliament for Derbyshire, and his eldest son, Mr. Curzon here mentioned was Nathaniel, who succeeded to the baronetcy on the death of his father in 1758, and was elevated to the Peerage in 1761 as Baron Scarsdale of Scarsdale, County Derby.

Lady Caroline Collyer, who was married to Mr. Curzon on October 27th, 1750, at May Fair Chapel, was the daughter of Charles, second Earl of Portmore.

The *Derby Mercury* of November the first of that year has the following record of the home-coming of the bride and bridegroom from London:—" This evening, between five and six o'clock, Nathaniel Curzon, Esq., with his newly married lady, and her father, the Right Honourable the Earl of Portmore, passed through this town in their coaches on their way to Kedleston, having been met some miles by Sir Nathaniel Curzon with his lady and a great concourse of persons on horseback, who attended them with loud acclamations to Keddlestone, where great preparations were making for their reception."

Lady Ferrers was the Baroness Ferrers of Chartley, in her own right, and married George, fourth Viscount Townshend, in 1751.

The Duke of Queensberry's eldest surviving son was Earl Drumlanrig, Member of Parliament for County Dumfries, who died unmarried in 1756.

Lord Egremont married, 1751, a daughter of George, second Lord Carpenter, and the title has since become extinct. It will therefore be seen that all these reports were incorrect, and none of the weddings spoken of were celebrated. Of Lord Exeter's two daughters one married, and the other remained single.

The co-heiresses of Thomas Tufton, sixth Earl of Thanet, married well.

Lady Betty Lewison—Lady Elizabeth Leveson—was fifth daughter of John, first Earl Gower, by his wife Lady Evelyn Pierrepoint, daughter of Evelyn, first Duke of Kingston. In 1751 she married Colonel John Waldgrave, and was sister to the Duchess of Bedford, and Lady of the Bedchamber to the Princess Amelia. She is often mentioned in Rigby's letters, and to her family she signed herself "Bettina."

Colonel Waldgrave succeeded his brother, in 1763, as third Earl Waldegrave.

This Lady Sackville was the wife of Lord John Sackville, second son of the first Duke of Dorset, and Frances, daughter of John, Earl Gower, and therefore was a connection of the Cokes. She appears to have been always known as "Lady Sackville."

Miss Shirley was probably sister of the Rev. Walter Shirley, and grand-daughter of the first Earl Ferrers.

Mr. Vernon was Henry Vernon, of Hilton Park, Staffordshire, a nephew of Admiral Vernon, married to Lady Henrietta Wentworth, daughter of Thomas, first Earl of Strafford of the second creation, in 1743. He was cousin of the Hon. Thomas Connolly. Horace Walpole mentions him thus :—" Do you remember a tall Mr. Vernon who travelled with Mr. Cotton ? He is going to be married to a sister of Lord Strafford."

This Mr. Connolly was the Right Honourable William Connolly, of Castletown, County Kildare, and Stratton Hall, County Stafford, Speaker of the House of Commons, and a Privy Councillor in Ireland. He was married to Lady Anne Wentworth, daughter of Thomas, third Earl of Strafford.

Mrs. Cornwallis was Mary, daughter of Charles, second Viscount Townshend. Her mother was Dorothy, daughter of Robert Walpole, of Houghton, Norfolk ; so she was a sister of the Minister, Sir Robert Walpole, and a cousin of Horace Walpole's, and became the wife of Edward, sixth son of the third Lord Cornwallis. He was Lieutenant-General Cornwallis, Member of Parliament for Westminster, Groom of the Bedchamber to King George II., and continued in the same office to the succeeding King, until he was appointed Governor of Gibraltar.

Horace Walpole incidentally mentions Mrs. Cornwallis's goodness of heart and tenderness as follows :— "You will be sorry to hear of Augustus Townshend's death. I lament it extremely, not so much for his sake, for I did not honour him, but for his poor sister Molly's, whose little heart, that is all tenderness and gratitude and friendship, will be broke with the shock."

Augustus Townshend was a Captain in the East

Indian Service, and died at Batavia, in Java, whilst in command of the *Augusta*.

Mrs. Cornwallis was a great friend of Lady Jane's, and they passed much of their time together at Windsor and elsewhere.

Miss Lovell may have been some connection of the Coke's, as one of Lord Leicester's titles was Baron Lovell of Minster Lovell.

Saville Row,
October the 9th, 1750.

I am quite ashamed to have received two letters from dear Mrs. Eyre, without having wrote, but you know I have been a great traveller, which must be my excuse. I passed my time very agreeably in the country and never remember so fine an autumn. I was a month with Lady Rockingham, and should not have left her so soon if I had not had business here. The unsettled way of life I have been in for many months makes me feel glad to be at home, though I am not yet settled; the changing houses I find a much more troublesome undertaking than I imagined, however I hope it will be quite finished this week. I wish I might flatter myself that there is any probability of dear Mrs. Eyre being in town this winter. If I was as absolute as the King of France I should order my subjects, whereas I doubt all I must pretend to is a remonstrance. Tell Mr. Eyre, with my best compliments, that if he could persuade you to come to town it would give me a very high opinion both of his eloquence and politeness; at present it is extremely empty, but people are coming every day. Sir Nathaniel has certainly great merit to his son, and I admire him prodigiously for letting Mr. Curzon please himself, without thinking of money. Lady Caroline is one of my beauties and very much commended; I suppose you will have some gaieties at Kedleston when she arrives; I should think your gold silk the handsomest on such an occasion. I am sure nobody would choose to buy clothes now silks are so excessive dear, the best plain damasks of common colours are eighteen shillings a yard, and I have given half-a-guinea for an unwatered tabby. There is no news but abundance of weddings, Lady Ferrers to the Duke of Queensberry's eldest son, and Lord Egremont has two given him, Lord Exeter's daughter and Lord Thanet's. I should think the last most probable. The town says Lady Betty Lewison is privately married to Colonel Waldgrave, but does not own it because of keeping her place. Lady Sackville is retired into the country, never to return. I am sorry to hear Miss Shirley is returned to Bath, and not settled as well as I wish her. I beg my best compliments to the family at Etwall. If Mrs. Cotton wants only a chair for a pattern, I think she cannot have a handsomer than one of my work at Longford that was made up in London and used to stand in the drawing-room, any of the servants that lived with me can tell which I mean, but if she had rather have one from hence, I will send her one when I receive her commands, and shall be glad to be employed.

In looking over my things I found your solitaire, which* extremely surprised me, as I thought I had sent it with Miss Cotton's things; will you order anybody to call for it, as it is too little to send any other way. You are very good to enquire after my health, which has been mended by the Tunbridge Wells waters, but I have been a good deal out of order these two days with the cholic, a complaint I never had so bad before, but whether sick or well I am always dear Mrs. Eyre's

Affectionate friend and humble servant,

J. COKE.

I hope Madam Sal: does not forget me. Mr. Vernon has let his house in town for three years to Mr. Conolly. Poor Mrs. Cornwallis is gone very ill to Bath. Miss Lovell is with her aunt.

LETTER XIV.

The relations between Lady Jane and her husband's successors appear to have been very strained, and from all we can gather they continued to remain so. She takes credit to herself for not having been in fault in the matter. This Mr. Coke was Wenman Roberts, son of Major Philip Roberts and of his wife Anne, a sister of Lady Jane's late husband, and he had taken the surname of Coke on succeeding, at his uncle's death, to the Longford estates and property. He married Miss Elizabeth Chamberlayne. His eldest son, Thomas William Coke, of Holkham, Member of Parliament for Norfolk, was created in 1837 Earl of Leicester, a title which had previously, in 1744, been bestowed upon his maternal great uncle, who was the elder brother of Mr. Robert Coke, Lady Jane's husband.

Gambling was then an all-pervading habit, and Thackeray in "The Four Georges," when writing about this reign (George II.), thus graphically describes the "ruling passion."

"When we try to recall social England, we must fancy it playing at cards for many hours every day." Gaming has become so much the fashion, writes Seymour, the author of the "Court Gamester," that "he who in company should be ignorant of the games in vogue would be reckoned low bred, and hardly fit for conversation. There were cards everywhere. It was considered ill-bred to read in company. But cards were the resource of all the world. Every night, for hours, kings and queens of England sat down and handled their majesties of spades and diamonds." "Books, prithee don't talk to me about books," said old Sarah Marlborough. "The only books I know are men and cards." One of the good old lady writers into whose letters I have been dipping cries out, " Sure, cards have kept us women from a great deal of scandal."'

The new farce alluded to was *Queen Mab*, commenced at Drury Lane the twenty-sixth of December, and continued all through the following January. It was described as a "new entertainment in Italian grotesque characters."

Arthur Murphy, the actor, relates that in 1751 "the play houses at this time had great attractions, Quin at Covent Garden, and Garrick at Drury Lane, drew crowded houses. There were besides Mrs. Cibber, Mrs. Pritchard, Mrs. Clive, and that excellent comedian, Harry Woodward."

Mr. Lamb, whose good luck is here mentioned, was Matthew Lamb, of Bracket Hall, Herts, afterwards created a Baronet in 1755. He married Charlotte, daughter of the Right Honourable Thomas Coke, of Melbourne, Derbyshire (teller of the Exchequer, and Vice-Chamberlain of Queen Anne), and eventually became the heir of her brother, George Lewis Coke. Sir Matthew Lamb, who represented Peterborough in three Parliaments, was one of His Majesty's Council for the Board of Trade, and custos rotulorum of the liberty of Peterborough, and died in 1768, and was succeeded by his son, Sir Peniston Lamb, who was elevated to the Peerage as Baron, and afterwards Viscount Melbourne; he was the father of Lord Melbourne, who became First Lord of the Treasury and Prime Minister on the resignation of Earl Grey, and with one intermission of 113 days remained in office for six years and nine months until 1841. Melbourne is a fine old place in Derbyshire, and is noted for its picturesque, old-fashioned gardens.

Horace Walpole refers in one of his letters to the dancer Auretti as follows:—"We are making great parties for the Barberina and the Auretti, a charming French girl; and our schemes succeed so well that the opera begins to fill surprisingly."

The Okeover family have been Lords of Okeover, in Staffordshire, on the borders of Derbyshire, for upwards of seven hundred years, from which place Ormas took his surname soon after the Conquest, and there his descendants have had their principal seat ever since.

The Okeover family at this time consisted of Leake Okeover, who died in 1763, aged sixty-three, and his wife Mary, who was a daughter of John Nichol, Esq.

The entertainments at Kedleston were of course in honour of the home-coming of the bride and bridegroom, Mr. and Lady Caroline Curzon.

Saville Row,
January the 19th, 1751.

I am quite ashamed to have been so long without returning my thanks to you, dear Mrs. Eyre, for the pleasure your letters always give me, but some business, constant airing (without which I am not well), and bad colds which nobody has escaped here, have prevented my writing. I hope you are all as well as I wish you, and then

I am very sure you will have no complaint; I am most extremely obliged for your kind invitation for the next summer, and should be very happy to see you, but as I am not invited to Longford I believe you will agree with me that it would not be right for me to be visiting in the neighbourhood. This I would not have talked of, because I am sure if Mr. Coke was left to act for himself he would always behave right to me, and as he is not I do not take it ill, but this I would not say to anybody but yourself. Since I have so much vanity to believe that I have some friends in Derbyshire that think I merit some civility from the Longford family, and would wonder if I did not meet with it, therefore I beg you will only say, if ever you are asked about my coming into Derbyshire, that I have not said anything to you of my having received an invitation to Longford, for I would not have it believed that I have been asked and refused coming. A consciousness of having acted right is a pleasure not to be taken from me, and I thank God I find that, and consequently am more indifferent how those behave who are obliged to me. As I shall always wish to preserve your good opinion, I thought it necessary to say thus much, which I hope will make you think it not my own fault that I do not accept your kind invitation. I am quite undetermined how I shall dispose of myself next summer. Another journey to Tunbridge, however disagreeable to me, will, I am afraid, be necessary for my health, and that at such a time of year as breaks into all my schemes. I have been vastly better for those waters, and as health is the first blessing, whatever procures that ought to be first considered ; but I believe you wish I would have done with my own affairs, and tell you a little of what is passing here. There is no news but what you see in the papers. Hitherto London has been very dull for young people, as there has been no balls nor any entertainment but cards, assemblies in abundance, and really the love of play seems the ruling passion of both sexes. Bragg flourishes as much as ever, and I believe ruins half the women in town. There is a new farce, so much commended that it even excited my curiosity to see it, and it really diverted me ; a dance of fairies by children, the oldest not seven, would surprise you. Operas are to begin next Saturday, but only at the Little Theatre, and very bad singers, so that I fancy they will not succeed. You have heard, I suppose, of Mr. Lamb's good luck ; his brother-in-law, Mr. Coke, dying without a will, the whole estate comes to him, so that he will be your neighbour at Melbourne; the dancer Auretti, who lived so long with Mr. Coke, has only one hundred pounds a year for her life, and some trifling jewels he gave her. Pray make my kindest compliments to Madam Sal:, and tell her I am very much obliged to her for her letter, and liked the verses extremely. The Okeover family dined with me the other day, and told me much Derbyshire news. I don't find the Kedleston entertainments were approved of; form seldom pleases. My best compliments attend Mr. Eyre, and I am very sincerely, dear Mrs. Eyre,

Yours affectionately,

J. COKE.

LETTER XV.

Lord Leicester, who was Sir Thomas Coke, K.B., of Holkham, was raised to the peerage as Baron Lovel of Minster Lovel, and was created Viscount Coke and Earl of Leicester in 1744. He married Lady Mary Tufton, the fourth daughter and co-heir of Thomas, sixth Earl of Thanet, and commenced the erection of that stately pile of buildings called Holkham Hall, but did not live to see it completed. He had an only son, Viscount Coke, who predeceased him. Upon his Lordship's death, his extensive estates devolved upon his nephew Wenman, who had assumed the name of Coke. Lord Leicester appears not only to have been very disagreeable to Lady Jane, but also to Lady Mary Coke, the wife of his son,

Viscount Coke, and the daughter and co-heir of John, Duke of Argyll and Greenwich; for Horace Walpole writes in 1752, "I now entirely credit all that my Lord Leicester and his family have said against Lady Mary Coke and her family." She was treated by Lord Leicester and his family with the greatest severity, although for an entirely different cause.

The Duchess of Wharton, as has been stated, was Maria Theresa O'Neill O'Beirne, maid of honour to the Queen of Spain, and daughter of an Irish officer in the Spanish service, and the widow of Lady Jane's ne'er-do-weel brother, the first and last Duke of Wharton, whose estates were attainted. The Duchess had been residing in London since her husband's death in 1731 in very reduced circumstances, and dependent upon a small pension allowed to her by the Spanish Government, as the English authorities do not seem to have recognised her claim to the income derived from the Duke's attainted property. Lady Jane must have been much relieved to have thus finally wound up her brother's affairs after a lapse of twenty years from the time of his death.

This Mr. Brydges was possibly Henry, a clergyman and Rector of Agmondesham, Buckinghamshire, who married a daughter of Sir Robert Atkyns, Lord Chief Baron of the Exchequer. Lady Jane was connected with the Brydges family (Dukes of Chandos), her maternal grandmother having been a daughter of John Brydges, Lord Chandos.

In Lady Jane's will, amongst bequests to her friends, appears the name of Mrs. Lucy Skipwith, to whom she leaves the sum of one hundred guineas; beyond this we have no further clue to her identity.

The *Gentleman's Magazine* states that Frederick, Prince of Wales, died at Leicester House, on March 20th,

1751, by the breaking of an abscess upon the lungs. "His Royal Highness is said to have caught a cold three weeks before in Kew Gardens, and to have increased it on the twelfth instant, by coming very warm from the House of Lords with the windows of his chair down. Soon after, he complained of pains which were thought to be pleuretic, and was attended with fever. The Prince had been in a declining state for some time, and was judged too weak to bear repeated bleeding, he was therefore blistered and thought to be out of danger. About a quarter of an hour before his death he told Dr. Wilmot, who had attended him and been up all night, that he was much better and advised the doctor to go home; the Princess, however, remained with him, and he soon after complained to her of a sudden pain and an offensive smell, and immediately threw himself back and expired. This excellent Prince, who is almost universally regretted with uncommon tenderness, was born at Hanover, January 20th, 1706, and on April 27th, 1736, was married to Her Most Excellent Princess Augusta, only surviving daughter of Frederick II., Duke of Saxe Gotha, by whom he left issue five sons and three daughters."

The *Gentleman's Magazine* also records the fact that the Princess of Wales, "who so eminently excels in everything that is truly admirable, has discovered an almost unexampled tenderness for His Royal Highness during his illness, and has never been in bed the whole time, notwithstanding she is in a delicate state, till this morning at six o'clock, and rose again at eight."

Horace Walpole writes about the King (George II.) and the Princess of Wales (after the death of the Prince of Wales) as follows:—" The King and Princess are grown as fond as if they had never been of different parties, or rather as people who always had been of different. She discountenances all opposition, and he all ambition. Prince George, who, with his two eldest brothers, is to be lodged at St. James's, is speedily to be created Prince of Wales."

Lady Curzon was Mary, daughter and co-heir of Sir Ralph Assheton, Bart., and wife of Sir Nathaniel Curzon, of Kedleston. Lady Caroline Curzon, as previously mentioned, was the daughter of Lord Portmore.

This time Lady Jane is correct in all her forthcoming wedding announcements. Lady Ferrers married Lord Townshend's eldest son. She was Lady Charlotte Compton, daughter of the Earl of Northampton and of his wife Elizabeth, Baroness Ferrers, of Chartley. She brought into the Townshend family upwards of 250 quarterings, including the royal one of Plantagenet, and inherited from her mother the Barony of Ferrers of Chartley, and from her father the Barony of Compton. Her husband was Charles, fourth Viscount Townshend, a Field-Marshal and Colonel of the 2nd Regiment of Dragoon Guards, and also a Privy Counsellor, High Steward of Tamworth, Yarmouth, and Norwich, Governor of Jersey, and Master-General of the Ordnance, and held the Lord Lieutenancy of Ireland from 1767—1772, and during which government Lady Townshend died at Dublin. She is not to be confounded with her mother-in-law, the more noted Audrey, Lady Townshend, wife of the third Viscount.

This Marquis of Rockingham was Charles Watson Wentworth, second Marquis. He married Miss Bright, but having no issue, all his honours at his decease, with the title, became extinct, the principal part of his estates devolving on his nephew, William, Earl Fitzwilliam. The Marquis was elected a Knight of the Garter in 1760, and in 1765 appointed First Lord of the Treasury, and sworn of the Privy Council, but held the Premiership only a single year, and was from that time leader of a strong party opposed to the measures of the Administration, until restored to office in 1782 in his former post of First Lord of the Treasury and chief of the "Rockingham Administration," of which Charles James Fox and Edmund Burke formed a part. He died the same year he returned to power. Miss Bright was Mary, daughter and co-heir of Thomas Bright, Esq., of Badsworth, Yorkshire.

Lord Coventry was William, sixth Earl, and his marriage took place in March, 1752.

Miss Gunning was the eldest of the two beautiful daughters of John Gunning, Esq., of Castle Coote, County Roscommon. Her youngest sister married the Duke of Hamilton in February, 1752, a month previous to her own wedding.

Horace Walpole often mentions Lady Coventry, and in July, 1752, writes: "It is literally true that a shoemaker at Worcester got two guineas and a half by showing a shoe that he was making for the Countess, at a penny a-piece."

We shall hear a little more of these two famous sisters in a later letter.

Mr. Shirley was the Rev. Walter Shirley, brother to Miss Shirley. He married Henrietta Maria, daughter of John Phillips, of Dublin, and was fourth son of Laurence Shirley and grandson of Robert, first Earl Ferrers; his three elder brothers were respectively fourth, fifth, and sixth Earls; he had also six sisters. He was the grandfather of the Right Rev. Augustus Shirley, D.D., Bishop of Sodor and Man.

Lady Cotton was Mrs. Eyre's sister, and the wife of Sir Lynch Cotton, and the mother of little Madam Sal:.

Saville Row,
May the 6th, 1751.

I would not begin a letter to dear Mrs. Eyre till I had time to write a long one. I am extremely obliged always to you and the family at Etwall, and am glad to find by your letter that Mrs. Cotton approved my reasons for not coming into Derbyshire this summer; however, these reasons are now at an end, for Mr. Coke and his whole family have taken their leave of me, and I now neither hear nor see anything of them; this behaviour to me is by Lord Leicester's order, who will not have anybody that expects favours from him live in friendship with me. This is the reason given, and I have long known there are very few in this age who will not give up every consideration to the single one of interest. Whether it is acting right or no, is another question. This I am sure of, that it does not hurt me, and I wish Mr. Coke may find his new friends as sincere to him as his old ones were.

He at least thinks it worth the trial, and I thank God none of the family can say we had ever the least obligation to any of them. I beg your pardon for taking up so much of your time upon so disagreeable a subject, but as it is no secret in town, I would not have it one in the country, therefore you may mention it to those you think proper. The weather here at present is more like November than May, which I am not sorry for, as I am kept in town by some business with the Duchess of Wharton; however, it is some comfort that it is the last thing we have to do, for I think I may venture to say my brother's affairs are at last finished. I go to Mr. Brydge's for a fortnight, and after that shall settle with Mrs. Skipwith for the rest of the year, but when I shall get out of town is uncertain; your letters directed to Saville Row will always find me. The death of the Prince put an end to all fashions, and I do not believe there will be any change in the mourning till they go into white gloves. The behaviour of the Princess in this melancholy occasion has been so proper, that I have not heard one fault found with her; the King is excessive good to her and fond of the children, who are all to live with her. I know no news but what the papers will tell you.

More people of fashion have died this year than ever I remember. Lady Curzon and I, met the last week at a great rout at Lady Rockingham's; she looks mighty well, but Lady Caroline sadly, which, I suppose, is her being with child. Mr. Meynell has dined with me, and seems as well as ever I saw him, and grown very fat. I wish you would have done like him and taken a trip to London this Spring, to have enlivened the rest of the year. I am sure my friend Mr. Eyre tried to persuade you; tell him if I did not think so, I would quarrel with him, but as I believe it was your own laziness that hindered your coming, I desire my best compliments to him. The weddings now talked of are Lady Ferrers and Lord Townshend's eldest son; the Marquis of Rockingham and Miss Bright, who is a vast fortune; and Lord Coventry and the eldest Miss Gunning, whose beauty you must have heard much of. I wish it may make her fortune, for I think generally speaking it is very little use, and oftener does our sex more harm than good.

I was very glad to be at home one morning when Mr. Shirley called, whom I saw at your house; he told me a great deal of Derby news and seemed in great spirits, I wish they would not be too good for the quiet life of a country clergyman; I heard of Miss Shirley from Bath this winter, and am afraid she is rather a finer lady there than either you and I thought her when she was with us at Derby.

I sent your solitaire to Lady Cotton's as you directed, and hope you will receive it safe. I shall expect to hear from you very soon, that I may know you excuse this long dull letter, from, my dear Mrs. Eyre's,

Yours most sincerely,

J. COKE.

Pray remember me very kindly to Madam Sal:, and make my best compliments to the family at Etwall.

LETTER XVI.

Lady Cobham was Hester Temple, daughter of Sir Richard Temple, Bart., of Stowe, and she, on the decease of her brother Richard, Viscount and Baron Cobham, a distinguished military commander under the great Duke of Marlborough, in 1749, inherited as Baroness and Viscountess Cobham, and was created Countess of Temple immediately after, with the reversionary dignity of Earl Temple to her heirs male. She married Richard Granville, Esq., of Wooton, Member of Parliament for Andover, and afterwards for the town of Buckingham, and at her death left several distinguished sons.

"Stowe is situated on an eminence rising gradually

from the lake. It covers a large extent of ground, and when beheld from a distance appears like a vast grove interspersed with columns, obelisks, and towers, which apparently emerge from a luxuriant mass of foliage. The gardens obtain their distinguished celebrity from the alterations effected by Lord Cobham, under whose direction the groves were planted, the lawns laid out, many of the buildings erected, and the corridor and wings added to the north front of the house. The gardens were begun when an affected regularity was the mode, when straight paths, canals, avenues, and fountains were considered both the greatest beauties; the formalities of art studiously displayed in every shape of monstrous deformity."—"Beauties of England and Wales."

"The suffering eye inverted nature sees,
Trees cut to statues, statues thick as trees."
POPE.

Horace Walpole in August, 1753, writes: "I have been here (Stowe) these two days extremely amused and charmed indeed. Wherever you stand you see an Albano landscape. Half as many buildings I believe would be too many, but such a profusion gives inexpressible richness."

Ranelagh, so called from its site having been that of a villa of Viscount Ranelagh, near Chelsea. The last entertainment given in it was the Installation Ball of the Knights of the Garter, in 1802. It has since been razed to the ground. The principal room, the rotunda, was first opened in 1742. It is thus described by Madame de Bocage on her visit to England :—" From Vauxhall let us take a step to Ranelagh. The gardens, which there have fewer ornaments, present to the eye a vaulted amphitheatre of a hundred feet diameter, and with three rows of seats in the midst of rural thickets; the floor is matted, which makes walking easy and agreeable; in the midst there is a furnace with four fronts, surrounded with a balustrade to which the heat penetrates without being excessive, and makes winter pass unnoticed. This magnificent enclosure pleased me so much, that I could not but prefer it to all the enchantments of Vauxhall. Though few are of my opinion, I can support it by good authority, that of the Earl of Chesterfield."

Horace Walpole mentions the place several times. "I have been breakfasting this morning at Ranelagh Garden, they have built an immense amphitheatre, with balconies full of little alehouses; it is in rivalry to Vauxhall, and costs about 12,000 pounds. The building is not finished, but they get great sums by people going to see it and breakfasting in the house; there were yesterday no less than three hundred and eighty persons at eighteenpence a head." And again, "Two nights ago, Ranelagh gardens were opened at Chelsea, the Prince, Princess, Duke, much nobility, and much mob besides, were there. There is a vast amphitheatre, finely gilt, painted and illuminated, into which everybody that loves eating, drinking, staring, or crowding, is admitted for twelvepence. The building and disposition of the gardens cost sixteen thousand pounds. Twice a week there are to be Ridottos, at guinea tickets, for which you are to have a supper and music. I was there last night, but did not find the joy of it. Vauxhall is a little better, for the garden is pleasanter, and one goes by water." At Vauxhall, Madame de Bocage remarks that "more women are to be seen here at assemblies, and at public diversions, than at Paris, and that there are entertainments of which we have no idea." She is "delighted with the gardens of Vauxhall, which are to be seen upon the delightful banks of the Thames. There in the morning the proprietor furnishes all comers with bread and butter, milk, coffee, tea and chocolate, beside music, for the small price of a shilling. In the evening there is an illumination, a concert, and all sorts of refreshments, but then the shilling is not sufficient, there is something to pay over and above. Sometimes there are balls for a guinea a head, and for this trifle all that repair to it are entertained in the most elegant manner; there are songs, dances, and masquerades, which in elegance equal anything to be seen at the Paris opera. The ladies never take off their masks. There are but few balls at the assemblies; persons of all ranks and ages come in a negligent dress from all quarters to soothe their cares by innocent amusement. The French look upon it as a phenomenon, that there should be so much order, and so profound a silence in the midst of such a multitude, whilst with us the smallest assembly occasions a stunning noise."

The mourning for the Prince of Wales being now over, Lady Jane turns her attention once more to fashions. The sacque was a wide loose gown open in front, and which hung from the shoulders to the ground, generally set in, by a wide pleat at the back and gathered in folds over the hooped petticoat. The hoops varied in size from small hoops for undress and larger hoops were worn in full dress, or as Lady Jane quaintly styles it, "when I am to be set out." The hoops were formed of whalebone, and the wearers doubled them round in front, or lifted them up on each side, when they entered a door or carriage. The hair was trimmed close round the face, which was encircled with curls, one or two falling behind, and surmounted by a little cap, similar to that immortalised by Mary Queen of Scots.

The following is from an advertisement of the time, of the loss of "a brocaded lustring sacque with a ruby-coloured ground, and white tobine stripes, trimmed with floss; a black satin sacque with red and white flowers, trimmed with white floss; a pink and white striped tobine sacque, and petticoat trimmed with white floss, and a night gown with a tobine stripe of green and white, trimmed with floss of the same colour, and lined with straw-coloured lustring."

Miss Margaret Nicholl was a niece of Mrs. Okeover, and is further alluded to in Letter XXIII.

Horace Walpole has something to say about this lady, and very much regrets the abortive efforts that were made to bring about a match between her and his nephew Lord Orford, whose pecuniary affairs were in a bad way. Walpole, says his friend Mr. Chute, "actually persuaded her to run away from her guardians, who used her inhumanely and are her next heirs. How clearly he is justified you will see, when I tell you that the man who had eleven hundred a year for her maintenance and education is gone to the Fleet."

Lord Orford was George, third Earl, who at this time had only succeeded two months to the title, on the death of his father. He sold the celebrated and magnificent gallery of paintings at Houghton, collected by his grandfather, Sir Robert Walpole, to Catherine, Empress of Russia, for the sum of £40,555. Amongst the pictures were the portraits of Lord and Lady Wharton by Vandyke. Lord Orford died unmarried in 1791, and he was succeeded in the title by his uncle,

Horace Walpole, the litterateur, from whose gossipy and contemporaneous letters we frequently quote passages.

Margaret, Countess of Orford, was the mother of the above-mentioned Lord Orford, and the daughter and sole heiress of Samuel Rolle, Esq., of Heanton, Devonshire. She eventually succeeded to the Barony of Clinton, and married secondly the Hon. Sewallis Shirley.

Horace Walpole remarks upon the match, "Lady Orford has picked up Mr. Shirley, no great genius," and Lady M. Wortley-Montagu in a letter to her daughter writes, "Statira (Lady Orford) has declared to her son that she is marrying Shirley, but ties him up strictly," and again, "I am not surprised at Lady Orford's marriage; her money was doubtless convenient to Mr. Shirley, and I dare swear she piques herself on not being able to refuse him anything."

Mr. Shirley was Sewallis Shirley, son of Robert, first Earl Ferrers and Comptroller of the Household to Queen Charlotte. He married Lady Orford at May Fair Chapel, and as she was the sister-in-law of Horace Walpole, he naturally has something to say about her new husband, and writes, "Mr. Shirley has had uncommon fortune in making the conquest of two such extraordinary ladies (Lady Vane and Lady Orford), as equal in their heroic contempt of shame, and eminently above their sex, the one for beauty and the other for wealth. He appeared to me gentle, well-bred, well-shaped, and sensible, but the charms of his face and eyes, which Lady Vane describes with so much warmth, were I confess always invisible to me, and the artificial part of his character very glaring."

Lady Anne Furnese was Lady Anne Shirley, sister

H

of Sewallis, and she was married to Sir Richard Furnese, Bart.

The Dowager Lady Ferrers was Selina, daughter of George Finch, Earl of Winchelsea, and widow of the first Earl Ferrers. Lady Mary Wortley-Montagu writes, "I have some curiosity to know how the pious Lady Ferrers behaves to her new daughter-in-law."

June the 21st, 1751.

I hope, my dear Mrs. Eyre, you will excuse my being so long without thanking you for your obliging letter; in London one's time is taken up unaccountably. I am now very quietly settled in the country, in a place I like extremely. We are but one mile from Windsor, and yet as retired as if it was a hundred miles from London. The Terrace and the Park at Windsor are allowed to be, and certainly are, the finest spots of ground in England; there we walk every evening that we are not disposed to go farther. There is the forest for airing, and a vast variety of fine places to see, all which are new to me. I am here with Mrs. Skipwith, which is vastly more comfortable than being alone. I hope you are all as well as I wish you. Lady Curzon and Sir Nathaniel gave us the kindest invitation that was possible to Kedleston for this summer, but my engagements were made so that I could not have the pleasure of accepting it, for I stay here till Michaelmas, when I have promised Lady Cobham to go to Stowe. Though London was very hot and disagreeable before I left it, there was many of my acquaintances in town, and, if I had chose it, parties for every evening. I was at Ranelagh and Vauxhall several times. The latter I like much the best, both from the place itself and the going by water to it, but I think Ranelagh is most in fashion; everybody is glad I fancy to get out of the dismal dress they have worn so long. You ask me whether sacks are generally worn; I am so partial to 'em that I have nothing else—a sack and apron, with a very small hoop, when I am undressed, and the whole ones when I am to be set out. The short caps you mention are only worn by young people who curl their hair after the French Ambassadress' fashion and is very difficult to do well. Why would not you give me some commissions? It would have given me great pleasure to have been employed by you, but I flatter myself you will come to town next winter and please yourself; I should be most extremely glad to see you, and can't find any one reason you can have against it. I was never more surprised than at all the bustles there has been in Mr. Okeover's family. I always thought her an extremely good sort of woman, and could have had no notion from their way of living of their running out in the manner they have done, Miss Nicholls I doubt must have something wrong in her temper, and on such occasions there is always much more said than is true; the ill-nature of the world generally aggravates misfortunes, but I think whatever cause Miss Nicholls had to be angry, she should have gone to her aunt since her distresses, which I hear she did not. Lord Orford has proposed to her, and is refused. Lady Orford is married to Mr. Shirley, and visited by his family; she has dined with Lady Anne Furnese and the Dowager Lady Ferrers, and they speak of her with great respect. The greatest part of her estate is in her own power, and 'tis said she will settle it on her son, and give Mr. Shirley only twenty thousand pounds.

I beg you will make my compliments to the family at Etwall, and am glad you showed Mrs. Cotton my last letter. I never hear anything from the Longford neighbours, if I had deserved such treatment as I have met with, it would make me uneasy, but I thank God I never thought any money could make up for the loss of friends, or being ungrateful; those who think otherwise I do not envy. I hope Mr. Eyre will remember his Queen as a dutiful subject ought; my best compliments attend him, and I am ever, my dear Mrs. Eyre,

Your sincere friend and humble servant,

J. COKE.

Remember me kindly to Madam Sal:. Pray write soon and direct for me as usual to Saville Row.

LETTER XVII.

Cliveden, in Bucks, was founded by George Villiers, Duke of Buckingham, and was at this time owned by Lady Orkney, and was the residence of the Prince of Wales. This noble building was burnt down in 1795. The estate has since passed through many hands, and is too well known to all passing up and down the Thames to need any further description.

Lady Orkney was Anne, daughter of Lord George Hamilton, raised to the peerage as Earl of Orkney. She was Countess of Orkney in her own right, and married the fourth Earl of Inchiquin, and died in 1756.

The Duke of Marlborough's "whimsical island" was Monkey Island in the Thames, and Lady Hertford, in a letter to her friend Lady Pomfret, thus describes it: "I went last week to see a little island which the Duke of Marlboro' has bought at Bray, and which, with the decorations, is said to have cost him eight thousand pounds. He has a small house upon it whose outside represents a farm, the inside what you please, for the parlour, which is the only room in it except a kitchen, is painted upon the ceiling in grotesque, with monkeys fishing, shooting, &c., and its sides are hung with paper. When a person sits in this room he cannot see the water, though the island is not above a stone's cast over; nor is he prevented from this by shade, for except six or eight walnut trees, and a few orange trees in tubs, there is not a leaf upon the island; it arises entirely from the river running very much below its banks. There is another building which I think is called a temple, but it rather gives one the idea of a market house. Upon the whole it should seem that his Grace has taken a hint from the Man of Ross's public spirit; and in order not to copy him too slavishly, has bestowed a treat upon the eyes of the passengers, rather than that he has proposed any enjoyment to himself, for he cannot move upon the island without being seen by all the bargemen who pass, neither can he get out of reach of their conversation if they are disposed to talk."

The Derbyshire election was in June, 1751, when Lord Frederick Cavendish was elected, *vice* his brother, Lord Hartington, called to the Upper House. Lord Frederick represented Derbyshire from 1751-54, and was then the Member for the town of Derby 1754-80. He was the third son of William, third Duke of Devonshire, and was born in 1729. He was a gallant soldier, had a distinguished military career, and voted for Wilkes, with his two brothers, who were also Members of Parliament; in 1767 he became a Lord of the Bedchamber to His Royal Highness the Duke of Cumberland, and died unmarried in 1803.

"The Longford Lady" was of course Mrs. Wenman Coke, wife of the nephew of Lady Jane's husband, who had succeeded his uncle in the property.

Miss Peggy Banks was Margaret, a daughter of Joseph Banks, Esq., of Hevesby, High Sheriff of Lincolnshire in 1736, and sometime Member of Parliament for Peterborough. She married in 1757 the Hon. Henry Grenville (fifth son of the Countess Temple), appointed Governor of Barbadoes in 1746, and Ambassador to the Ottoman Porte in 1761.

Horace Walpole relates that "the Countess of Orford happened one night at the opera, to sit by Peggy Banks, a celebrated beauty, and asked her several questions about the singers and dancers, which the other naturally answered as one woman of fashion answers another. The next morning Sir Bourchier Wrey sent Miss Banks an opera ticket, and my lady sent her a card to thank her for her civilities to her the night before, and that she intended to wait on her very soon." This Walpole calls "an excellent vulgarism which has entertained the town," and says "Do but think of Sir B. Wrey's paying a woman of fashion for being civil to my Lady O.! Sure no apothecary's wife in a market town could know less of the world than these two people!" and once more alluding to the subject he says, "The Grenvilles and Peggy Banks design to appear and avow their triumph" (at Sir William Stanhope's party, at Aylesbury Races), and he also mentions that in 1746 "the Duke of Cumberland gave his ball last night to Pegg Banks at Vauxhall. When they came to Vauxhall there were assembled about five and twenty hundred people, besides crowds without. They huzzaed and surrounded him so that he was forced to retreat into the ballroom."

Mr. Hodgkinson was Robert Banks, who on the death of his father took the name of Hodgkinson on succeeding to his maternal grandfather's estate, his mother having been the only daughter and heir of William Hodgkinson, Esq., of Overton, in the county of Derby.

The beautiful valley of Dovedale had its admiring parties of tourists and visitors even in those days, though they were very few in comparison to the hordes of noisy trippers and holiday-makers who daily throng there during a greater part of the year at the present time. It is "a romantic and rocky chasm through which the river Dove pursues its winding course, and gives life and animation to the scenery by dashing over the rude masses that have fallen into its stream from the adjoining cliffs. On entering the dale the mind regards it as a sequestered solitude. As the road proceeds the scenery becomes romantic and impressive from its singularity. The valley contracts; and on each side, rocks of grey limestone, abrupt and vast, rear their grotesque forms, covered with moss, lichens, yew trees, and mountain ash. A narrow and broken path winds along the margin of the river, which in some parts so nearly fills the bosom of the Dale that even the foot passenger cannot pursue his cautious way without the hazard of being precipitated from the slippery crags into the stream. The length of the Dale is rather more than two miles. The rugged, dissimilar, and frequently grotesque and fanciful appearance of the rocks distinguish the scenery of this valley from, perhaps, every other in the kingdom."—" Beauties of England and Wales."

Lady Jane again twits Mr. Eyre with his love for Derbyshire scenery, and when she mentions " nothing embellishes a view more than seeing one's own land " she alludes to Mr. Eyre's estate of Rowtor in North Derbyshire.

Evidently Mr. Eyre had heard some rumours of Lady Jane's remarrying, which she intimates are false, and that after two experiences of matrimony she has no intention of again giving up her liberty.

July the 26th, 1751.

My dear Mrs. Eyre,

As I had much rather be thought very dull than one moment forgetful of my friends, I choose not to defer thanking you for your obliging and entertaining letter, though I know not the least news to send you in return; I am at present much more acquainted with places than people, not that there wants company at Windsor, or we visitors, but as I am not fond of new acquaintances, I do no more than civility requires. If I was to give you an account of all the pretty places I have seen in this neighbourhood I should tire you extremely. Cliveden I like the best, though I saw it with the disadvantage of all the Prince's furniture being taken away, you know he rented it of Lady Orkney; don't tell Mr. Eyre that I think the prospects from the gardens equal at least, if not superior, to any in his favourite country. It stands very high, a steep cliff covered with shrubs, and the Thames running at the bottom, and looks over the most beautiful country I ever saw, interspersed with great variety of houses, villages, and woods; the Duke of Marlborough has a very whimsical island just by us, which pleases me extremely from its singularity. It is in the middle of the Thames—several flowering shrubs, and about ten old walnut trees, which are shade enough, two very ornamental buildings, one where the people live that look after it, with a parlour and bedchamber for the Duke, the other an extreme good room, with a delightful prospect of the river, &c.; but I believe by this time you wish I had done my descriptions. I am glad you had so quiet an election, as I know you don't love bustles better than I do. Lord Hartington has a great deal of merit I do believe, but one may say he is lucky. Pray did the Longford Lady appear at the Assembly? I want to know if she goes much about, for I never hear anything of them, nor would I ask anybody but dear Mrs. Eyre. I should have thought poor Mrs. Ward's dancing days had been over, but I am sure 'tis right to be diverted as long as one can. You had like to have had some visitors of my sending. Miss Peggy Banks and her brother Hodgkinson were at Ashbourn to see Dovedale, and would have come to Derby, but 'twas at the time of the Election and they could not get lodgings; if they had they would have waited on you. They were at Okeover, and she writes me word it is said Mr. Okeover will have fifteen hundred a year left when his affairs are settled. I wish it may be true, and if it is I think it a great pity there should have been so much said. Will Blowzabella ever part with her place of Lady of the Assembly? I own I doubt it much, because when she does she must make up the accounts, and to so fine a lady that would be very troublesome and disagreeable. I rejoice to hear you intend coming to London. I shall depend on the pleasure of seeing you, therefore will not admit of any excuses when the time comes. My very best compliments attend the family at Etwall. I shall execute any commission Mrs. Cotton sends me with great pleasure. Tell Miss Cotton I congratulate her on a conquest I hear she has made in her neighbourhood; the power of her charms must be very great since she has made him a poet. I shall answer my subject's postcript, and am ever, dear Mrs. Eyre,

Yours most sincerely,
J. COKE.

My kindest services to Madam Sal:.

P.S.—Lady Jane allows Mr. Eyre to like the prospects in the Peak better than those from Windsor, because nothing embellishes a view more than seeing one's own land. As to the report he has heard, she takes it for granted he cannot believe it, as she is very sure he thinks it much better to govern than obey, therefore desires he will not imagine his Queen intends parting with her present sovereignty, but behave like a dutiful subject and give her some account of Blowzabella, hops, &c., &c.

LETTER XVIII.

Mr. Cotton was Rowland Cotton, Mrs. Eyre's father.

The Queen of Denmark was the youngest daughter of George II., and is alluded to by Horace Walpole in 1746 thus:—"Princess Louisa has already reached the object of her wish ever since she could speak, and is Queen of Denmark." The poor Queen enjoyed her position but a few years, and her death on December 8th, 1751, is thus alluded to in the *Gentleman's Magazine*:— "About the middle of this month died His Majesty's (George II.) youngest daughter, the Queen of Denmark, a princess of great spirit and sense, and in the flower of her age," after an operation which lasted an hour. The King was much grieved, and broke into expressions of passion and tenderness, exclaiming: "This has been a fatal year to my family. I lost my eldest son, but I am glad of it, then the Prince of Orange died, poor little

Edward has been cut open (for an imposthume in his side), and now the Queen of Denmark is gone. I know I did not love my children when they were young, I hated to have them running into my room, but now I love them as well as most fathers."

The "King certainly goes abroad in April." George II. frequently went to his kingdom in Hanover. Thackeray writes:—"He is always going back to Hanover. In 1729 he went for two whole years, during which Queen Caroline reigned for him in England, and he was not the least missed by his British subjects. He went again in 1735 and 1736, and between the years 1740 and 1755 he was no less than eight times on the Continent, but was obliged to give up at the outbreak of the seven years' war."

Mr. Fitz-Herbert was either William Fitz-Herbert, Recorder of Derby, who, by his industry and economy, retrieved the family estates which had suffered so materially in the Civil War; or his son William, who was His Majesty's housekeeper at Newmarket, and became Member for Derby in 1762 till 1772.

Mademoiselle de la Touche, or as she is styled in the letter Madame de la Touche, was a natural daughter of Monsieur Bernand, the Paris banker. The Duke of Kingston fled with her to England, and a prosecution for the abduction was commenced before the Parliament of Paris in 1737, but the French King put a stop to it. The Duke lived with the lady many years, but deserted her finally for Miss Chudleigh.

Lady Juliana Collyer was the daughter of the second Earl of Portmore, and the sister of Lady Caroline Curzon. She married in 1759 Henry Dawkins, Esq., Member of Parliament, of Standlynch, Wiltshire, and

Over-Norton, Oxfordshire. There was also at one time a rumour that she (Lady Juliana) was going to marry Lord Granville, who was a widower and considerably her senior, and Horace Walpole says she is "a very pretty girl," and that "there are not above two or three-and-forty years difference in their ages. If this should turn out true I can't help it."

It was a very great pleasure to me, hearing from dear Mrs. Eyre. I was almost afraid you had quite forgot me, as I had wrote a long while ago, and never had an answer. I sincerely rejoice to hear Mr. Cotton is recovered, and desire you will assure the family at Etwall they will always have my best wishes. If they go to Bath I hope they will come by London, that I may have the pleasure of seeing them, but why do you say nothing of your journey, spring is approaching, and I hoped you were determined to come? I wish Derby was not quite so distant from hence; the disuse of travelling makes one lazy, and though I should be vastly happy to be in Derbyshire again, for this summer I have given up the thoughts of it, and have taken a house at Windsor for the six months, and hope to go thither the latter end of April. I have been here ever since the middle of September, and am quite satisfied with cards and assemblies. Mrs. Cornwallis has promised to be with me, and though a ready-furnished hired house is quite new to me, yet it is a pretty situation, and the finest country I ever saw; I hope it will do very well. I am surprised to find you did not mourn for the Queen of Denmark, as I thought Derby too genteel to be out of the fashion; 'tis almost as universal here, and to the full as deep, as for the Prince of Wales; it is not yet determined whether black gloves will be left off till March. The King certainly goes abroad in April, so that the mercers will have little to do. I thank dear Mrs. Eyre for all the news you sent me, and wish I could tell you any in return, but I really know none. I hope Mr. Fitz-Herbert is out of danger. Poor Madame La Touche is, I think, to be pitied, she must suffer extremely. The newspapers marry the Duke to Lady Juliana Collyer, but I hear there is not the least foundation for the report, and the town says he is rather engaged in a flirtation than a matrimonial affair. I have seen Mrs. Wilmot, who is surprisingly recovered since last year. Miss Shirley and I have visited, but never met; by what I hear Bath has done her no service; the other morning her brother was here in his canonical habit, and looked extremely decent. Mr. Hodgkinson has no thoughts of going abroad, but I believe his heart failed him to settle so far from London as Derby, which made him part with his house there. I do not wonder at anything I hear of the lady who put out her kitchen fire, and should imagine, where every consideration gives way to interest and the love of money, 'tis very likely an object with them to save coals even in Derbyshire. Pray let me hear from you very soon, and believe me, my dear Mrs. Eyre,

Yours most sincerely,

J. COKE.

My respects to Mr. Eyre and love to Madam Sal:.

Saville Row, January the 28th, 1752.

LETTER XIX.

Mrs. Eyre had been paying a visit to town, and evidently much appreciated the delights of Ranelagh and Vauxhall, which Lady Jane seems to infer she was reluctant to leave.

The journey from London to Derby in a lumbering postchaise must have occupied three or more days, as this was some thirty years before the time of the *fast* mail coaches and improved roads. Glover mentions that a coach "left the George Inn at Derby and the Bell Inn, in Holborn, London, every Thursday, and performed the journey in three days (if God permit)."

Lady Jane mentions the beauties of Windsor, the river on one side and the castle on the other. She must have often walked on the castle terrace, from whence Pope describes the view in the following lines:

> "Here hills and vales, the woodland and the plain,
> Here earth and water seem to strive again,
> Not chaos-like, together crushed and bruised,
> But, as the world, harmoniously confus'd,
> Where order in variety we see
> And where, tho' things differ, all agree."

Lady Mary Coke, who was on a visit to Lady Jane at Windsor, was Lady Mary Campbell, fifth daughter of John, second Duke of Argyll and Greenwich, and in 1747 became the wife of Edward, Viscount Coke. Her marriage was not a happy one. In reading her letters (privately published), one sees that she was a very vain and exacting lady, and therefore it is probable she required constant attention, and took up a great deal of Lady Jane's time.

Horace Walpole in 1746 writes: "I can tell you of another wedding as certain and fifty times more extraordinary; it is Lord Coke with Lady Mary Campbell, the Dowager of Argyll's youngest daughter. It is all agreed, and was negotiated by the Countess of Gower and Leicester. . . . It's a strange match. After offering him to all the great lumps of gold in all the alleys of the city, they fish out a woman of quality at last with a mere thousand pounds."

Sir Edward Hulse, who attended Miss Cotton for smallpox, was one of the leading physicians in London, and first physician to George II., by whom he was made a baronet in 1738. The same year he purchased Braemore in Hampshire, which is held by his successors in the title. He is described as one of the Whig doctors, and is said to have differed so seriously with Freind over the case of Lord Townshend that he withdrew, declaring his lordship must die if Freind had his way. (Townshend recovered, having declared he would live or die by the hands of Freind.) In his old age Sir Edward was possessed of the idea that he would die of want, a fear which his attendants overcame by putting guineas regularly into his pocket, where he used formerly to deposit his fees. He died in 1759.

The "orange" mentioned as being extremely good was evidently a Seville orange preserved whole in syrup, for which there is a recipe in an old cookery book of the Cotton family.

Windsor,
May the 1st, 1752.

I was extremely glad to hear dear Mrs. Eyre arrived safe at home, and daresay, notwithstanding the pleasures London affords, you were rejoiced to find yourself quietly seated in your own dressing-room, though 'tis above an hundred miles from Ranelagh and Vauxhall. I don't wonder you were tired of a post-chaise, for I think it a terrible conveyance. Though my journey hither was not quite so long as yours, yet I was in a bustle some time before. I have been here a fortnight to-day, and at last am settled for the summer, at least I hope so, for I don't intend to see London unless business calls me. Lady Mary Coke has been with me a week, and entirely took up my time, or I should sooner have thanked you for your obliging letter. Mrs. Cornwallis is now here to stay some months, and though the weather is much more like November than May the day passes very agreeably. This house is but indifferent, the situation delightful, the Thames runs at the bottom of the garden, and the other side is the view of Windsor Castle, which I had rather look at than inhabit, it is so very much exposed. I had wrote thus far when I received Madam Sal:'s letter. I am extremely concerned to hear of Miss Cotton's illness, though I hope by this time you are out of pain about her, and then 'tis a good thing over. I am glad she has Sir Edward Hulse, as I have always heard he is particularly skilful in the small-pox. Assure Madam Sal: I am so pleased with her correspondence that the first morning I have time I will write her a letter of thanks, and answer my subject. In the meantime tell Mr. Eyre I am his most Gracious Princess, for though he would not come to see me at my Court, I hope to visit him in his Principality, where I know his power is absolute. I went to Russell's the day before I came out of town, and he would neither show me your cross and ear-rings nor tell me what they come to; I shall be glad to know what he makes you pay for the setting. You can't mistake in putting the ribbon to it, and as to the length, you may either wear the cross upon your neck, or the bottom of it to touch the top of your stays; the roses you may send for at any time.

A thousand thanks for the box, which came very safe, and the orange is extremely good. I have some letters I must write to-day, therefore can only add that I am ever, my dear Mrs. Eyre,

Yours most sincerely,

J. COKE.

Direct for me at Windsor in Berkshire.

● LETTER XX.

Lady Jane is enjoying the delights of the country near Windsor, where she can either remain in retirement or indulge in the pleasures of society.

The Installation was the chief event that had taken place, and it may be of some interest to give the names of those who were installed Knights of the Garter at Windsor, on June 4th, 1752. They were H.R.H. Prince Edward Augustus, by his proxy, Sir John Ligonier; H.S.H. the Prince of Orange, by his proxy, Sir Clement Cotterel-Dormer, Kt.; and the Earls of Lincoln, Winchilsea, and Cardigan. "The ceremony, which lasted from eleven to half an hour after twelve, was performed by the Dukes of Marlborough, Kingston, and Portland, after which an elegant entertainment with a fine desert representing in confectionery all the devices of the Order of the Garter. In the evening was a grand ball in the Castle for the ladies, which was opened between nine and ten by the Earl of Lincoln and Lady Caroline Petersham; about twelve the company retired to supper, and afterwards returned to dancing till between three and four; there was a most brilliant appearance of the nobility and gentry of both sexes. The populace attempted several times to force their way into the hall where the knights were at dinner, against the Guards, on which some were cut and wounded, and the Guards fired several times on them with powder to deter them, but without effect, till they had orders to load with ball, which made them desist."

Lady Winchilsea and Mrs. Finch were the two daughters and co-heirs of Sir Thomas Palmer, and married two brothers, as alluded to in the introduction to Letter XII.

The Duke of Kingston was Evelyn Pierrepoint, the second duke. His aunt, Lady Mary Wortley-Montagu, appears to have had her doubts of how he would grow up, for she writes: " The Duke of Kingston has hitherto had so ill an education 'tis hard to make any judgment of him; he has spirit, but I fear will never have his father's good sense." She was not mistaken, for he afterwards became notorious for his profligacy, and married the shameless Miss Chudleigh, whose trial for bigamy by the House of Peers is well known, and dying without issue in 1773, all his honours became extinct.

Miss Chudleigh was the daughter of Colonel Thomas Chudleigh, Lieutenant Governor of Chelsea Hospital, second son of Sir George Chudleigh of Ashton, in Devon. She was born in 1720, and at twenty-one years of age she came to London, and was appointed Maid of Honour to the Princess of Wales. Her wit and beauty attracted many admirers, and she had an offer of marriage from the Duke of Hamilton. Her relations intercepted and destroyed the letters the Duke wrote her, and she was led to believe that he had forgotten her. Under these circumstances she became an easy prey to a young and handsome lieutenant, Augustus John Hervey, afterwards third Earl of Bristol, whom she had met at the Winchester races, and a private marriage took place late one night. Mr. Hervey returned to his ship, which was ordered to the West Indies, and Miss Chudleigh to her position as Maid of Honour, taking up her residence in Conduit Street. On two occasions Mr. Hervey returned to England ; but the marriage was kept a secret, and a violent quarrel taking place between them they parted, and never saw each other more. Later the same year (1747) a son was born, but his birth was kept a secret, and he soon afterwards died. "The vivacity and indiscretion of the lady were at least equal to her beauty, and soon after her parting with her husband she set decency and decorum at defiance, and appeared at a masquerade in the character of Iphigenia, almost in the unadorned simplicity of primitive nature."

For several years she indulged in hours of dissipation and revelry, but with the departure of youth sordid passions took possession of her, and after twelve years' absence from her husband, the infirm state of Lord Bristol's health seeming to open up the prospect of a rich succession and a title, she adjusted the proof of her marriage with Mr. Hervey. Shortly after this she formed a connection with the Duke of Kingston, and instead of acceding to her husband Mr. Hervey's wish to make up their former disputes, she instituted a suit of jactitation of marriage, and obtaining a sentence which it was thought would be sufficient to bar any claims of her husband in future, she married the Duke of Kingston, at St. George's, Hanover Square, in March, 1769, and lived with him until 1773, when he died leaving her a life interest in his estates. The Duke's relations resented this, and determined on revenge. They resorted both to the civil and criminal courts, and the Duchess fled the country, but was obliged to return to avoid outlawry.

The Earl of Bristol died in 1775, and the Duchess's first husband (Mr. Hervey) succeeded to the title, which at all events gave her the privilege of a peerage. The next year her trial by the House of Lords for bigamy took place at Westminster Hall, which was thronged with a regal and aristocratic audience, and after a five days' trial she was found guilty, receiving, however, the benefit of her peerage, in spite of pains to the contrary, and was discharged on paying the fees, and without the stigma of burning in the hand. She left England and went to live in France, where she purchased an estate at St. Assize, near Paris, abounding in rabbits of superior quality, and she thereupon turned rabbit merchant. In 1788, at the age of sixty-eight, hearing a lawsuit in France had gone against her, she flew into a violent rage, burst a blood-vessel, and expired a few days afterwards alone and unmourned.

Windsor,
June the 12th, 1752.

Dear Mrs. Eyre,

I was extremely glad to hear Miss Cotton was so well recovered, and hope you have had the pleasure of meeting your whole family well at Etwall. The weather is now vastly fine, and the country in its greatest beauty; though I had promised to go for a day and see some of my friends before they went out of town, I broke my word, and have not seen London since the second week in April. Mrs. Cornwallis and I work and read in the heat of the day, and every evening go out either in the coach or by water. The good of this situation is, one may be as much retired as one pleases, and if I have an inclination for company, here are some very agreeable people. I like this place so well that I have offered either to take a very long lease or buy it, but my landlord will not part with it. We have been much enlivened by the Installation, which brought a great many of my acquaintances to Windsor; Lady Winchilsea did the honours. I did not intend to see any part of the show, but she and Mrs. Finch made me go to the ball, and when I was there I liked it extremely, there were so many rooms in the castle opened, and very well lighted, and there was no crowd. They danced in two rooms, several sideboards for lemonade and ice, tea, and coffee; all kinds of dessert-things and a supper at twelve o'clock. There was two tables, one had sixty covers, the other thirty, and everything was extremely well ordered; you will easily imagine there was a great deal of finery, as everybody that went to the choir were quite dressed. The Duke of Kingston was one of the assistant knights; he came from London but that morning, and was so fatigued that he was forced to take drops during the ceremony; he only stayed to dine with the knights and set out from hence before the ball. Miss Chudleigh was not here, she has been very ill, and was not enough recovered to venture; I am really sorry for Madame,* an absolute retirement will not do for those who do not carry with them innocence and peace of mind. I am very glad Mr. Russell has acquitted himself so well; he certainly sets neater than anybody. When you have your cross, ear-rings, and roses on, you really will be well dressed enough for an Installation. I wish the amusements at Derby would improve, by your account at present they are but bad.

I foresee the end will be, Blowzabella's getting the better of everybody but the Lady of Radbourne. Pray make my best compliments to Mr. Eyre; remember me kindly to Madam Sal: ; and believe me always,

Yours sincerely and affectionately,
J. COKE.

My best wishes attend the family at Etwall.

* Madame de la Touche.

LETTER XXI.

Lady Jane has again been at Tunbridge for the benefit of her health, and appears to have found it more agreeable than upon her former visit, when she was in too deep mourning to indulge in the amusements and "hurries" she now alludes to. She is glad, nevertheless, to find herself back at her favourite abode near Windsor.

Lady Guildford was the third wife of Francis, first Earl of Guildford, and was Katherine, Countess Dowager of Rockingham, and daughter and co-heir of Sir Robert Furnese, Bart. Her stepson, Lord North, was Prime Minister from 1770-1783, and her residence in Oxfordshire was Wroxton Priory, near Banbury, the extensive manor of the Earl of Guildford, which was erected on the site of the ancient Augustine priory, the greater part by Sir William Pope, afterwards Earl of Downe in 1618; the estate came into the North family by the marriage of Francis Lord Keeper Guildford with Lady Frances Pope, sister of the fourth and last Earl of Downe. "The Earl of Guildford built a fine chapel and library. The house contains many portraits of the Pope and North families; of the latter there was a complete series from the first Lord North to the Earl of Guildford. Every improvement introduced has remained subservient to the ancient baronial character of the edifice, and no innovating hand has robbed the gardens and grounds of their monastic features."—"Beauties of England and Wales."

The Act of Parliament referred to was one passed in 1751, licensing all houses of entertainment, and making it penal to allow gambling or disorderly behaviour therein.

We have already alluded to Richard Nash, the notable leader of fashion, or Beau Nash, as he was usually called, and now quote some verses written in the highflown and artificial style of the period on his illness at Tunbridge Wells, mentioned in this letter.

> " Say, must the friend of human kind,
> Of most refin'd—of most diffusive mind ;
> Must Nash himself beneath these ailments grieve :
> He felt for all—he felt—but to relieve,
> To heal the sick—the wounded to restore,
> And bid desponding Nature mourn no more.
> Thy quick'ning warmth, O let thy patron feel
> Improve thy springs with double power to heal
> Quick, hither, all-inspiring Health, repair,
> And save the gay—and wretched from despair ;
> Thou only Ezra's drooping sons canst cheer,
> And stop the soft-ey'd virgin's trickling tear ;
> In murmurs who their Monarch's pains deplore,
> While sickness faints, and pleasure is no more ;
> O let not death with hasty strides advance,
> Thou, mildest Charity, avert the lance ;
> His threatening power, celestial maid, defeat ;
> Nor take him with thee, to thy well-known seat ;
> Leave him on earth some longer date behind,
> To bless, to polish, and relieve mankind :
> Come then, kind health ! O quickly come away
> Bid Nash revive—and all the world be gay."

Lady Anne Hamilton was a daughter of the fifth Duke of Hamilton and Brandon, and married in 1761, Arthur, first Marquess of Donegal.

Horace Walpole in 1750 writes :—" The housekeeper (Mrs. Marriot) at Windsor is dead. The revenue is large (£800 a year) and has been largely solicited. Two days ago at the drawing room, the gallant Orondates (George II.) strode up to Miss Chudleigh and told her he was glad to have an opportunity of obeying her command, that he appointed her mother (a widow) housekeeper at Windsor, and hoped she would not think a kiss too great a reward. Against all precedent he kissed her in the circle. Her life, which is now of thirty years' standing, has been a little historic."

With reference to the small-pox and inoculation, Lady Mary Wortley-Montagu writing from Constantinople mentions that " Apropos of distempers, I am going to tell you a thing that I am sure will make you wish yourself here. The small-pox, so fatal and so general amongst us, is here entirely harmless by the invention of ingrafting, which is the term they give for it. There is a set of old women who make their business to perform the operation every autumn, in the month of September when the great heat is abated. People send to one another to know if any of their family has a mind to have the small-pox ; they make parties for this purpose, and when they are met (commonly 15 or 16 together) the old woman comes with a nut shell full of the matter of the best sort of small-pox, and asks what veins you please to have opened. She immediately rips open that you offer to her with a large needle (which gives you no more pain than a common scratch), and puts into the vein as much venom as can lie upon the head of her needle, and after binds up the little wound with a hollow bit of shell ; and in this manner opens four or five veins. The Grecians have commonly the superstition of opening one in the middle of the forehead, in each arm, and on the breast, to mark the sign of the cross ; but this has a very ill effect, all these wounds leaving little scars, and is not done by those that are not superstitious, who choose to have them in the legs or somewhere that is concealed. The children or young patients play together all the rest of the day, and are in perfect health to the eighth. Then the fever begins to seize them, and they keep their beds two days, very seldom three. They have very rarely above 20 or 30 in their faces, which never mark ; and in eight days' time they are as well as before their illness. Where they are wounded, there remain running sores during the distemper, which I doubt is a great relief to it. Every year thousands undergo this operation, and the French ambassador says pleasantly, that they take the small-pox here by way of diversion, as they take the waters in other countries. There is no example of any one that has died in it, and you may believe I am very well satisfied of the safety of the experiment, since I intend to try it on my dear little son."

I hope my dear Mrs. Eyre remembers that I have been at Tunbridge and then she will excuse my long silence, for any sort of application gives the headache, and there is not an hour unemployed. I drank the waters five weeks, and they have done my stomach a vast deal of good. Several of my particular acquaintance being there, made the place more agreeable to me than it would other ways have been, but notwithstanding that, I found myself very glad to quit the hurries I lived in at Tunbridge for the quiet I enjoy at Windsor, where I am now settled for some time. The only excursion I shall make this year will be to see Lady Guildford in Oxfordshire, I wish Derbyshire was as near, but I do not give up the hopes of visiting you there, though it is a long journey. I want extremely to know how Mrs. Cotton and you will all do, for I think it a great while since I had the pleasure of hearing from you. I hope this fine summer has contributed to mend Mrs. Cotton's spirits, for let the Methodists preach ever so well I shall always think that whilst we are in this world our constitution will affect the strongest minds. She wanted Lady Huntingdon's letter less than anybody, as she had more resolution than any person I ever saw which can come only from religion; but I suppose you'll expect some account of Tunbridge. It used to afford abundance, but this season has not produced even a lampoon, no beauties, and the Act of Parliament that has put a stop to publick gaming prevents a great many young mens' coming. Poor Nash has had a fit, but does not seem to mind it, though he looks just a-going. Miss Chudleigh was there a fortnight, so altered, I was surprised to see her by daylight. Lady Ann Hamilton was not with her, who since the small-pox has no remains of beauty but in her own opinion. The Duke of K. (Kingston) was always with them, that is a surprising affair, we are so used at Windsor to their coming together here to her mother, who is housekeeper, that now 'tis scarce mentioned.

I had a letter last post from your neighbour, Mr. Meynell. He was then at Aix-la-Chapelle, much better for the spa-water, and intends returning to England next month. I hear your assembly at the races was very empty. What is become of Blowzabella and her consort?

You are vastly good to think of giving yourself the trouble of sending me so many things. I liked the orange extremely, and wish you could give me any employment here, as for fashions there are too many to describe, at least for me who have done following them, and therefore do not mind their changes. My best wishes will always attend Mrs. Cotton. I hope dear Mrs. Eyre believes me her

Affectionate and obliged
J. COKE.

Windsor, August the 13th, 1752.

My compliments to Mr. Eyre, who I doubt in so long an absence forgets his obedience to his old Sovereign. Remember me to Madam Sal:, to whom I send the enclosed. If she has never seen it, she will be puzzled to read it, as good a scholar as I know she is.

LETTER XXII.

The following letter requires no comment, as it is short and speaks for itself, being merely a friendly reproof to Mrs. Eyre for not having given Lady Jane the pleasure of hearing from her.

What is become of you, my dear Mrs. Eyre? I wrote to you before I went my journeys, and have vainly expected the pleasure I always have when I receive a letter from you. I should have feared some illness had prevented your writing, had I not heard by Mr. Hodgkinson when I was at Stowe, about three weeks ago, that he called at your house, and that you were abroad and well. I won't suppose it laziness, but believe a letter has miscarried, and that I shall hear from you in answer to this, and beg you will direct it to Saville Row, tho' I am still at Windsor, and have not fixed my time for going to Lady Guildford's; the weather is so fine, and this place still in such beauty, that I cannot resolve to leave it. I wont tell you a word of news, as I mean this only a letter of reproof. However, I must desire my best compliments to Mr. Eyre and Madam Sal:, and assure you of my being, dear Mrs. Eyre,

Yours most sincerely,

J. COKE.

October the 11th, 1752.

LETTER XXIII.

Mr. Brydges is probably the same individual who is previously mentioned in Letter XV., and was a connection of Lady Jane's on her mother's side.

Sir Willoughby Aston, of Risley, Derbyshire, was member of Parliament for Nottingham in 1759, and married Elizabeth Pye, a niece of Lord Bathurst.

Blowzabella (Mrs. Barnes) at this date seems to have somewhat reluctantly resigned her post as patroness of the assembly, which she had held for eleven years, to Lady Ferrers. She had allowed the accounts to get into a terrible muddle, and evidently was obliged to make good the loss from her own purse. All this occasioned a great deal of talk and comment at Derby.

George, the third Duke of St. Albans, married Jane, daughter and co-heir of Sir Walter Roberts, Bart., of Glassenbury, Kent, and died without issue.

There were two Miss Nicholls who were heiresses. The first here alluded to was Frances, daughter and co-heiress of Sir Charles Gunter Nicholl, K.B., and her rumoured match with Lord Pulteney did not come off, as he ran away with another lady just before the wedding day. She afterwards, in 1755, became the wife of William Legge, second Earl of Dartmouth.

William, Viscount Pulteney, was the only son of Lord Bath, and died in 1763 during his father's lifetime. About his not marrying Miss Nicholl, Walpole writes: "I know nothing else but elopements. Lord Bath has lost his only son (Lord Pulteney), who is run away from thirty thousand pounds a year, which in all probability would have come to him in six months. There has

K

been some great fracas about his marriage; the stories are various on the *why*. Some say his father told Miss Nicholl that his son was a very worthless young man; others that the Earl could not bring himself to make tolerable settlements; and a third party says that the Countess has blown up a quarrel in order to have his son in her power and at her mercy. Whatever the cause was, this ingenious young man, who you know has made my Lady Townshend his everlasting enemy by repeating her histories of Miss Chudleigh to that *Miss*, of all counsellors in the world, picked out my Lady Townshend to consult on his domestic grievances. She with all the good nature and charity imaginable immediately advised him to be disinherited. He took her advice, left two dutiful letters for his parents to notify his disobedience, and went off last Friday night to France."

Mrs. Okeover's niece was Miss Margaret Nicholl, daughter and sole heiress of John Nicholl, of Southgate in Middlesex, and she married James Brydges, Marquis of Carnarvon, afterwards third Duke of Chandos. Mrs. Delaney describes her as "a fine, lively girl, but wants a good deal of modelling." Her affair with Lord Orford is alluded to in Letter XVI.

Lord Ferrers was Laurence, fourth Earl. He married on the 16th September, 1752, Mary, youngest daughter of Amos Meredith, Esq., the son of Sir William Meredith, Bart., of Hanbury, Cheshire. He was a man of ungovernable and violent temper, and in one of his paroxysms of rage put to death his land steward, named Johnson, in 1760, for which offence he was tried by his peers and condemned to suffer death. His wife married secondly John, fourth Duke of Argyll.

These "two Mr. Curzons" were the sons of Sir Nathaniel Curzon; the eldest Nathaniel, his heir, became Baron Scarsdale, and the second Assheton was created Viscount Curzon. Sir Nathaniel had no other children but these two sons.

Princess Amelia was the second daughter of George II., and died unmarried. She met Walpole at Bath, who conveys messages from her in a letter to Lord Hertford. "Princess Amelia told me t'other night she had seen Lady Massarene at Bath, who is warm in praise of you," and ends his letter with other messages from Lady M——. Lady Massarene was Elizabeth, daughter of Henry Eyre, Esq., of Derbyshire, by his first wife, and was therefore a stepdaughter of Mrs. Eyre. She was the second wife of the first, and mother of the second Earl of Massarene. Lord Massarene was married to Miss Eyre at St. Peter's Church, Derby, on November 25th, 1741, which was a general fast day. The *Derby Mercury* of November 27th has an epigram upon this in which the following lines occur:

> TOM: "What news friend Will; I've read the *Post*,
>   Didst hear of naught beside!"
> WILL: "This morn has made our Darling toast
>   A Lady and a Bride."

I am extremely obliged to you my dear Mrs. Eyre for your letter, and beg you will believe I would not have been so long without inquiring after you, but that I expected to have heard from you every post. Whoever had my letter will know a great deal of me, for I wrote just before I left Windsor, and gave you a full account of my intended travels. I was from home near five weeks, and passed my time very agreeably, the first fortnight I was at Mr. Brydge's, whom you must have seen at Longford, he has some neighbours that belong to Derbyshire and were at the Assize Assembly, the persons I mean are Sir Willoughby and Lady Aston, I did not see them but heard they gave a wonderful account of Blowzabella, and the management of the Assembly. People must love bustles extremely, to behave as she does, since I don't hear any more is desired of her, than to pay the money and be at quiet, Barnes's head must be quite turned, or he would not let her make him so ridiculous. Pray what does Mr. Eyre say on this occasion, because he and I used to agree in our opinions of Mr. Barnes, and now I do not think we can commend his understanding? I went from Mr. Brydge's to Stowe, which with the present possessors must always be a most agreeable place to be at. We were all in such good spirits as to go twice to a play acted by strollers in a barn, and were extremely diverted. I have been at Windsor these three weeks, and intend going to London and being settled in Saville Row for the winter next Friday. May I venture to own to you that I leave this place with infinite regret, but my landlord asks such an exorbitant price, that I cannot afford to keep it, so that I am again entirely unprovided with a place for next summer, but 'tis a great while before I shall want one, and I certainly intend making you a visit. I believe I shall find London a greater solitude than Windsor, here are frequent assemblies and I might be engaged at cards every evening if I chose it. The Duke of St. Alban's brings home his bride to his house here to-morrow, she is a great fortune but no beauty; both the Miss Nicholl's are gone, one to marry Lord Pulteney, and Mrs. Okeover's niece, Lord Carnarvon— the Duke of Chandos's son.—Lord Ferrers I find has despised money and I wish he may not find the want of it, I've heard from several people Miss Shirley made the match. What end could it answer to her? I must ask you if a story I was told in a visit here is true, which is that the two Mr. Curzon's quarrelled to such a degree about a horse that they do not speak to one another. I think it seems too ridiculous to be anything but a made story, if it is not I should be very sorry, as it must make Sir N. and Lady Curzon unhappy, and they certainly have great merit to their children.

I am much concerned at the account you give of Mr. and Mrs. Cotton's health, but hope he will find the same benefit he did last year from the Bath, which is made very gay by Princess Amelia's being there, I shall be glad to hear how Mrs. Cotton bore the journey, as you say nothing of your sister, I conclude she is very well, my best wishes attend Mr. Eyre who I hope is by this time quite recovered, as for Madam Sal: tell her I think she grows lazy, or I should have had a letter from her in all this time.

Adieu my dear Mrs. Eyre, believe me

• Ever affectionately yours,

J. COKE.

Windsor, October the 22nd, 1752.

Have the Longford family been at the assembly?

LETTER XXIV.

If Lady Jane has been so far north as Scarborough we have no record of her journey. She again alludes to the idea prevalent at that time that it was prejudicial to hold down the head after drinking mineral waters.

Lady Caroline Harpur was the daughter of John, second Duke of Rutland, and was at this time the widow of Sir Henry Harpur, a connection of Mrs. Eyre's.

A very bad cold in my head and eyes, and

some business with lawyers has prevented my returning dear Mrs. Eyre thanks for the many good things she sent me, the goose came perfectly sweet, and the quince is the best I ever eat. I don't intend this by way of letter, for I have been drinking Scarborough water and dare not hold down my head, but was resolved you should hear by this post that I am well, and extremely sensible of the obligations I have to you. Have you no commissions I could execute for you here? To be employed by dear Mrs. Eyre would be a real pleasure to

  Your most affectionate and obliged
          J. COKE.

November the 21st, 1752.

My best compliments to Mr. Eyre and Madam Sal: You shall hear from me soon. Lady Caroline Harpur's match that you mention as certain, is strongly denied by all her friends here.

LETTER XXV.

Evidently the final adjusting of her brother's (the Duke of Wharton) affairs took a longer time than Lady Jane expected.

"The Birthday of Her Royal Highness the Dowager Princess of Wales was celebrated as usual, and there were great courts at Leicester House and St. James's on Thursday November 30th."—"Gentleman's Magazine."

"New clothes on the birthday were the fashion for all loyal people. Swift mentions the custom several times. Walpole is constantly speaking of it; laughing at the practice, but having the very finest clothes from Paris nevertheless."—"The Four Georges," Thackeray.

Lady Betty Germain was Lady Elizabeth Berkeley, daughter of Charles, second Earl of Berkeley. She married the notorious adventurer and gambler, Sir John Germain, who had previously married the divorced Duchess of Norfolk, by whose bequest he became possessed of the estate of Drayton in Northamptonshire, which he left on his death in 1718, to Lady Betty his second wife, and she left it on her decease in 1769, to Lord George Sackville, third son of the first Duke of Dorset. Lady Betty was the friend and correspondent of Swift, and survived her husband fifty-one years. Sarah, Duchess of Marlborough spitefully describes her as "ugly without a portion," but by her friends she was considered charming and cultured.

Lady Pomfret in a letter to Lady Hertford writes, "The Duke of Marlboro' lost seven hundred pounds, twelfth night, which was all that was considerable: the Duchess of Dorset and Lady Betty Germain both played."

Lord Sydney Beauclerk being very handsome, almost persuaded Lady Betty in her old age, to marry him; but she was dissuaded by the Duke of Dorset and her relations.

In speaking of Drayton, Lady Betty's place inherited from her husband, Walpole, who often visited there, calls her "its divine old mistress. If one could honour her more than one did before, it would be to see with what religion she keeps up the old dwelling and customs, as well as old servants, who you may imagine do not love her less than other people do," and he also mentions that Drayton "was the old mansion of the Mordaunts, and is crammed with whatever Sir John could get from them and the Norfolks."

Lady Coventry, wife of the Earl of Coventry, had been only married nine months, she was the elder of the two beautiful Miss Gunnings.

Lady Caroline Petersham was the daughter of Charles, Duke of Grafton, she married Lord Petersham, afterwards Earl of Harrington. Walpole calls her and her two sisters "the three beauty Fitzroys," and writes, "Lord Petersham was married last night to one of our first beauties, Lady Caroline Fitzroy"; Mr. Chute wrote an epigram on her—

> "Who is this?
> Her face has a beauty, we must all confess;
> But beauty on the brink of ugliness:
> Her mouth's a rabbit feeding on a rose;
> With eyes—ten times too good for such a nose!"

Mrs. Watson had been married three months previously to the Hon. Lewis Monson Watson, brother to Lord Monson; she was the second daughter of Henry Pelham, Esq.

Probably "the Queen Mother" was as Walpole tells us "Lord Carteret's mother, whom they call 'the Queen Mother,' from taking upon her to do the honour of her son's power," and elsewhere he calls her "plump Carteret." She was Frances, daughter of Sir Robert Worseley, and first wife of John, Lord Cartaret, afterwards Earl of Granville, and died in 1744, shortly after her son's marriage to Lady Sophia Fermor.

A stomacher was a covering for the breast, of cloth, velvet, or silk, over which the bodice was laced. From the time of the Restoration to 1790 the stomacher was a conspicuous portion of female dress, and was covered with jewels.

It is evident that Madame Sal: is becoming a good French scholar and very likely she has given Lady Jane a proof of this in some of her letters.

My time has been so very disagreeably employed with lawyers almost ever since I came to town, that I have been hindered writing any letters but on business, or else I am sure dear Mrs. Eyre would have heard oftener from me. However, I hope this winter will finish all my brother's affairs, and when that is the case I shall be very happy. I'm glad for your sake Derby is grown so gay. Lady Ferrers has undertaken in my opinion a difficult task if she means to compose all differences about the Assembly. Madam Barnes is full as extraordinary a personage in London as by the Brook side. Would you believe she did not honour me with one visit? Barnes called several times when I was not at home. At last I sent him a card to say I would be glad to see him the next morning; he came, was in great spirits, but quite lame, assured me nobody in Derbyshire regretted our loss half so much as he did, and that if I had been anywhere within twenty miles of London he would have come to see me, but said nothing from Madam but her compliments; nothing is extraordinary she does. London is at present emptied against the holidays. There was more finery at the Birthday than ever I saw; don't imagine I was at Court, but I went to Lady Betty Germain's, where great numbers came to show themselves. Lady Coventry, Lady Caroline Petersham, and Mrs. Watson (who was Miss Pelham) were allowed the finest; their clothes had all silver grounds and coloured flowers with silver mixed, and a great quantity of jewels in their hair. Mrs. Watson had a diamond bird, with the wings stretched out, and in its beak held a diamond drop; her necklace comes down in rows and covers her neck. New fashions I am bad at remembering. However, one is so remarkable it is not easily forgot, which is a variety of Vandyke handkerchiefs; they are not worn in a full dress, and the prettiest are those made exactly after a picture of the Queen Mother. I would send you one, but they can't be well made without trying. Great numbers of different sorts of stomachers, and in short all sorts of finery that looks like great plenty of money and vanity. I hope you've had a good account from Bath. My best compliments to Mr. Eyre, and believe me ever my dear Mrs. Eyre,

Yours most sincerely,
J. COKE.

Saville Row, December the 23rd, 1752.

The enclosed card be so good to give the little French woman, Madam Sal:.

LETTER XXVI.

Lady Jane is again staying at Wroxton Priory, Lord Guildford's place in Oxfordshire.

This Mr. Vernon was George Venables-Vernon, of Sudbury, who was Member of Parliament for Derby from 1754 until he was raised to the Peerage as Lord Vernon in 1762.

The celebrated Duke of Cumberland was Ranger of Windsor Forest at this time, having received the wardenship on the death of the Duke of St. Albans in 1751, and his house is now known as Cumberland Lodge.

The piece of water mentioned is Virginia Water, which is an enlargement of the "Greene Pond" represented in a survey by Morden, made in the reign of James I. On the Duke's death in 1765, the rangership of the great Park was bestowed upon his nephew, the Duke of Cumberland, a brother of George III.

Pope writes of Windsor Forest:—

> "Waving groves a chequer'd scene display,
> And part admit, and part exclude the day."

Blenheim is the modern appellation of the Honour of Woodstock, which appertained for many years to the Crown, and was granted by Queen Anne to the celebrated Duke of Marlborough, with £500,000, wherewith to build a palace, which magnificent structure was designed by Vanbrugh. The demesne appendage to the Castle is 2700 acres in extent enclosed by walls, the gardens contained 200 acres of decorated pleasure grounds, and the lake, covering 250 acres, is described as an "august and lovely spread of artificial water."

Viscount Coke was the only son of the Earl of Leicester, member for Harwich. He was very extravagant, and dissipation hastened his end, and released his wife from incessant persecution at his and his father's hands. At the time of his marriage, Lady Mary Wortley-Montagu writes: "I knew him when he was at Venice, and believe her economy will be a very necessary ally to the expensiveness of his temper." Horace Walpole in 1748 says: "Lord Coke has demolished himself very fast. You know he was married last Spring; he has lost immense sums at play, and seldom goes home to his wife till eight in the morning. The world is vehement on her side, and not only her family but his own give him up. At present matters are patched up by the mediation of my brother, but I think can never go on. She married him extremely against her will;" and Lady Harvey writes: "The news wrote me of Lord Coke and Lady Mary was very near being quite true; but things are patched up for the present at least; in my opinion, whenever they want so much darning they seldom last long. Lord Leicester has once more pay'd his son's play debts, which are very considerable; and has made up the difference between the Lady Mary and him, which, I believe, was rather a more difficult affair; and he has in return got a promise that Lord Coke will for the future be fonder both of his money and his lady, and in short reform his whole conduct, which, by what I have heard, very much wanted it in every respect."

Lady Mary Coke, the youngest daughter of the second Duke of Argyll, married Lord Coke much against her inclinations. Her married life was a very unhappy one, and her quarrels with her husband and father-in-law were notorious, and almost became the subject of a disagreeable law suit, the differences being, fortunately for all concerned, settled on the day of trial. Walpole mentions that Lady Mary made her husband "a declaration in form that she hates him; that she always did, and that she always will. This seems to have been a very unnecessary notification. However, as you know, his part is to be extremely in love, he is very miserable upon it." In the "Letters and Journals of Lady Mary Coke" it is stated that "her beauty was by some allowed, by others disputed, the dissentients declaring she was neither more nor less than a white cat, from the dead whiteness of her skin, unshaded by eyebrows, and the fierceness of her eyes. She was very egotistical, nothing ever happened to her after the fashion of other people, not to mention the unprecedented behaviour of any man, woman, or child, she had anything to do with. She could not be caught in a shower of rain but it was such a rain as never before fell from the skies. No Turkish Prince yesterday living immured in the Seraglio, and to-day placed upon the Ottoman throne ever experienced a more agreeable change of situation and prospects than Lady Mary, when Lord Coke's excesses, producing an early decay, brought him to the grave only three years after their separation. At six-and-twenty she emerged from a very dull retirement and state of constant humiliation and fear into the perfect freedom of an independent widow, with a jointure of twenty-five hundred pounds a year, fully equivalent to what five thousand would be at present. Re-entering the world with the advantage of its good opinion, for she had been generally pitied, and everybody but a few friends of the Leicester family rejoiced at her deliverance. She conciliated further goodwill by her decent behaviour on the occasion; not affecting a concern she did not feel, but wearing mourning and abstaining from amusements for the usual space of time."

Horace Walpole was at one time supposed to be going to marry Lady Mary Coke, and often alludes to her, allowing that he was susceptible to her charms, and calls her a handsome young widow, and says he is afraid of going to Paris where Lady Mary happened to be, "the air of Paris works such miracles, that it is not safe to trust oneself there," and again "my heart is faithful to Lady Mary." " Half-a-mile from thence (Amiens) I met a coach and four with an equipage of French, and a lady in pea-green and silver, a smart hat and feather, and two suivantes." . . . . " My heart whispered that it was Lady Mary Coke." " Apropos to my wedding day, Prince Edward (afterwards Duke of York) asked me at the opera t'other night when I was going to marry Lady Mary Coke." I answered, " As soon as I get a regiment, which, you know, is now the fashionable way." Lady Mary fancied herself in love with the Duke of York, and now and then, in the belief that she was married to him, signed her name like a royal personage. She preserved to a very advanced age the cheerfulness for which she had been distinguished in her youth, and died the 30th October, 1811, surviving her husband fifty-eight years.

Lady Temple wrote a complimentary portrait of her as follows :

> " She sometimes laughs, but never loud,
> She's handsome too, but sometimes proud.
> At court she bears away the bell,
> She dresses fine and figures well ;
> With decency she's gay and airy ;
> Who can this be but Lady Mary."

A very fine old mulberry tree is still growing in the garden at Etwall, and the syrup of mulberries was evidently made from the fruit of this tree. There is a tradition in the Cotton family that whenever a large branch of this tree falls to the ground, it presages the death of a member of the family.

Your letter, my dear Mrs. Eyre, found me at Lord Guildford's in Oxfordshire, where I passed a fortnight very agreeably, and stayed there till the day they set out for Mr. Vernon's in Derbyshire, where they pressed me extremely to have gone with them, but I thought it so late in the year, that I should not have had time to have seen you before the rains came, and the roads grew bad, it has now proved otherwise, for I never saw finer weather, and though I am quite alone I don't begin to think of London. I walk as much or more than you remember I used to do at Longford, and this is by much the finest country for airing I ever saw. This morning I have been at the Duke of Cumberland's Lodge, to see his new works which are magnificent beyond description; a piece of water some miles in length, and in proportion broad, the banks of which are extremely beautiful. Upon this water are several boats, one large vessel, and what I went particularly to see is a Chinese ship, which is by far the prettiest thing I ever saw, with one very good room in it, and no expense spared in the finishing; he employs a hundred labourers every day, and has done so for some time. In my journey back from Lord Guildford's, I was at Blenheim, which did not answer my expectation; Oxford pleased me much better. You find I have been a great traveller, and now my journeys are over for this year, I hope to take one to Derbyshire some time or other, but will never promise you again so long beforehand, lest I should be disappointed. My employment since my return to Windsor has been to look for a habitation that I could either buy or take a long lease of, but to no purpose. We are genteel enough to have Assemblies here, but I never go to them, yours I hope flourish now Mrs. Barnes can make no quarrels, I don't wonder she likes going to Bath or anywhere from Derby. Poor Lord Coke's death, though it did not concern me, yet made me moralise, when I reflected how very different his character was at his first coming into the world, to what it was at his leaving it. Lady Mary has now two thousand pounds a year rent charge, and absolute mistress of herself, which at her age is no unpleasant situation ; your neighbour at Longford is now very likely to succeed to the whole family estate, and if money is happiness, he will have enough, and yet whether his spirits were not so good when he danced with you years ago, I much question.* What you say of Mrs. Coke is I believe extremely just, I doubt both she and Miss Ward will not improve by the air of Longford. I am extremely obliged to you for the good things you intend me, but I need not trouble you for any syrup of mulberries having enough left of last year's. By way of news, I know none that would amuse you. Miss Chudleigh is still a nominal Maid of Honour, she was here near a fortnight, and the Duke of Kingston with her, and happened to be taken very ill, when he sat up all night with her, and the apothecary of this town. We can talk at Windsor, as well as at Derby, therefore you may be sure we were not silent on such an occasion.

I rejoice to hear Mrs. Cotton is so well, my best wishes always attend her, and compliments to Mr. Eyre and Madam Sal:.

Believe me, my dear Mrs. Eyre,

Your obliged and affectionate,

J. COKE.

Windsor, October the 9th, 1753.

LETTER XXVII.

Mrs. Vernon, of Sudbury, was the wife of Mr. Vernon, member for Derby, who was afterwards raised to the peerage as Lord Vernon.

Regarding burlettas in 1748, Walpole writes: "The burlettas are begun; but, I think, not decisively liked or commended yet, their success is certainly not rapid." However, the comic operas appear to have improved, as in 1753 the same authority says, "The operas succeed pretty well, and music has so much recovered its power of charming, that there is started up a burletta at Covent Garden, that has half the vogue of the old "Beggar's Opera." Indeed, there is a soubrette, called the Niccolina, who besides being pretty, has more vivacity and variety of humour than ever existed in any creature," and again "There are no less than five operas every week, three of which are burlettas; a very bad company, except the Niccolina, who beats all the actors and actresses I ever saw for vivacity and variety."

Blake Delaval, of Seaton Delaval, Northumberland, had the misfortune to break his leg, which occasioned his death, the 14th November, 1752. His estates of £9000 a year devolved upon his eldest son, Member of Parliament for Hindon, who, perhaps, is the Delaval mentioned here.

The following lines called "Receipts for Modern Dress," published in 1753, give a good idea of the dress of this period.

> "Hang a small bugle cap on, as big as a crown,
> Snout it off with a flower, *vulgo dict*, a pompoon;
> Let your powder be grey, and braid up your hair
> Like the mane of a colt to be sold at a fair.
> Before for your breast, pin a stomacher bib on,
> Ragout it with cutlets of silver and ribbon.
> Your neck and your shoulders both naked should be,
> Was it not for Vandyke, blown with Chevaux de frize
> Let your gown be a sack, blue, yellow, or green,
> And frizzle your elbows with ruffles sixteen;
> Furl off your lawn apron with flounces in rows,
> Puff and pucker up knots on your arms and your toes;
> Make your petticoats short, that a hoop eight yards wide
> May decently show how your garters are tied.
> With fringes of knotting your dickey cabod,
> On slippers of velvet, set gold *a la daube*;
> But mount on French heels when you go to a ball—
> 'Tis the fashion to totter and show you can fall;
> Throw modesty out from your manners and face,
> *A la Mode de François*, you're a bit set for 'his grace.'"

Lady Northumberland was Elizabeth, the only daughter of Algernon, seventh Duke of Somerset, who had been created Baron Warkworth and Earl of Northumberland with remainder to his son-in-law Sir Hugh Smithson, who, on the decease of his father-in-law in 1750, succeeded to the honours limited to him, and was afterwards in 1766 created Earl Percy, and Duke of Northumberland.

Lady Carnarvon, the wife of John, Marquess of Carnarvon, was Lady Charlotte Tollemache, daughter of Lionel, the second Earl of Dysart. She had two sons and two daughters; the eldest of the latter married firstly, William Berkeley Lion, of the Horse Guards, and secondly, Edwin Francis Stanhope, a descendant of the first Earl of Chesterfield. The youngest daughter, a posthumous child, married her cousin, James Brydges of Pinner. Lady Carnarvon died in January, 1754; her mother was the daughter and heir of Sir Thomas Wilbraham from whom she probably inherited a large fortune; her only surviving sister, who married Sir Robert Cotton, of Combermere, died in 1748, without issue, and her sole brother Lord Huntingtower having died as far back as 1712, Lady Carnarvon was left to inherit all her mother's fortune.

Sir Marmaduke Wyvill, the sixth Baronet of Constable Burton, Yorkshire, was appointed Post-Master General of Ireland, 1736, and had married in 1716, Carey, daughter of Edward Coke of Holkham, Norfolk, and sister to the Right Honourable Lord Lovell, but dying without issue was succeeded by his nephew. He was Lady Jane's brother-in-law, and she was in complimentary mourning for him.

I don't think I should make any excuses to my dear Mrs. Eyre for my long silence, she does not deserve it, if she remembers how very long she was in answering my last letter. However, all animosities apart, I really want to know how you do.

I have been almost long enough in London to be tired of it, for though I pass so much of my life here, I always rejoice when the spring comes, that I may get into the country. Don't think the amusements I meet with makes me so bad a correspondent, but I have a great deal of disagreeable business, and go out every morning for my health, which takes up my time. I met Mrs. Vernon at Lady Guildford's, who is very well but vastly big; she told me that Lady Curzon has left off visiting her, and that she has not seen the Radbourn family this year, so that I find my old neighbours are not very sociable. Such changes will happen, and I have lived too long in the world to wonder at anything. We have variety of diversions this winter in town, operas, burlettas, (which are comic operas) are much admired, but I am so unfashionable to dislike them extremely. However, the girl that sings in them has charmed the Duke, but he has a powerful rival in Mr. Delaval, who declares he will give her his whole estate rather than lose her. You see what important affairs employ our great people here. Plays are in great perfection at Drury Lane, and my favourite diversion. As for fashions in dress, which you sometimes inquire after, they are too various to describe. One thing is new, which is, there is not such a thing as a decent old woman left, everybody curls their hair, shews their neck, and wears pink, but your humble servant. People who have covered their heads for forty years now leave off their caps and think it becomes them, in short we try to out-do our patterns, the French, in every ridiculous vanity.

Lady Northumberland gave an entertainment last week, in which was an artificial goose in her feathers, and a hen with seven little chickens. The desert was a landscape, with gates, stiles, and cornfields, but I have, I'm afraid, tired you with the account of such follies. Lady Carnarvon's immense riches are at present another subject of conversation. She made no will, and they have found above ninety thousand pounds. It comes between her two daughters, the eldest is married to a Mr. Stanhope, who has no fortune of his own, and the youngest one has been disordered in her head, is unmarried, but now very well. I must now have done telling you news, but can't end this without desiring my kindest compliments to Mrs. Cotton and Miss. I hope Mr. Eyre does not quite forget me, and that you will always believe me,

Yours most affectionately,
J. COKE.

My compliments to Madam Sal:. I am in black gloves for Sir Marmaduke Wyvill, but forgot black paper and wax till this minute. Pray let me hear from you very soon.

Saville Row, January 31st, 1754.

LETTER XXVIII.

We often imagine now-a-days that the springs have grown colder, but they appear, however, to have been as rigorous a hundred and fifty years ago.

A rout was what would now be called an "At Home" held in the evening.

The celebrated Madame de Bocage thus describes London of the period. "The town is dirty and ill paved, and the reason assigned for this is, that in a free nation citizens pave as they think proper, each before his own door; it is often necessary to break up the pavement in order to mend the pipes; all the houses in London are furnished with water from the Thames or the New River. The ladies are carried in sedan chairs within the barrier where passengers walk. In the evening two rows of lamps, which hang upon posts, give light, and make a gay appearance. The houses have half a storey under ground; this obliges people to ascend a few steps to come to the street door, which is exceeding narrow. It is the same thing with regard to the courtyard, where coaches can seldom enter, and therefore put up in a lane behind the house. The footmen wait by a fireside at the bottom of the stairs. There is no anti-chamber before the saloon where the company meets, which is adorned with little glasses, and has generally a closet belonging to it. About a dozen buildings which are here called palaces, but at Paris would pass only for large houses, and which men of fortune amongst us would find many faults with, are highly esteemed in London; but there are many large squares that have something very grand in them. To tell the plain truth, though there is great luxury in England, it does not come up to ours, which the people of this country imitate nevertheless, as all the nations of Europe do to their destruction.

There are scarce any arm-chairs in their apartments; they are satisfied with common chairs. The women who use no paint and are always laced are fond of these seats; in their court dresses they resemble the pictures of our great-grandmothers, but they are extremely affable and obliging in their behaviour."

March the 16th, 1754.

I am always very glad whenever I have the pleasure of hearing from dear Mrs. Eyre; you are but lazy, or would write oftener, considering how much time you have. The weather for these four last days has been, I think, colder than ever, and a deeper snow than has been known in London for some years. There is no stirring from the fireside; I thank God I've escaped colds better than usual this winter, and am very glad to hear Mrs. Cotton has borne the severe weather so well. I think her extremely in the right to change the scene by coming to Derby, which by your account has been more lively than usual. You should have been in the fashion, and had a rout; there is no end of them here at this time of year, and I dislike them almost as much as Mr. Eyre does. However, I think whilst one lives in the world, its customs must be complied with, or else retire, as Barnes and his fair consort have done. It is so cold I cannot hold my pen much longer, therefore must hasten to tell you my schemes for the approaching summer, which, if they meet with your approbation, I hope nothing will hinder their being put in execution. I propose making you and Mr. Eyre a visit the latter end of May, or the beginning of June, and if you'll be troubled with me, making your house my home whilst I stay in Derbyshire; and I beg dear Mrs. Eyre will tell me sincerely if that time will be agreeable to you. I have got a Prebend's house at Windsor, which I like very well, and shall be settled there when I come from you. If you have anything to do here I hope you know it would be a pleasure to me to be employed by you. My best compliments attend Mr. Eyre, and tell him I think the verses very pretty. Adieu, believe me,

   Your affectionate and obliged,

      J. COKE.

Remember me kindly to Madam Sal:. My letter should have been longer, if 'twas not so cold that I can write no more.

LETTER XXIX.

The two following letters are brief, and relate principally to shopping and commissions, as the two friends are to meet so shortly.

Lute-string was a corded silk then much worn, and sold at 13s. the yard.

Mrs. Manroi was a French milliner. Dressmakers were called mantua-makers in those days.

Mrs. Egerton was probably related to the Cheshire Egertons of Tatton, as a member of that family lived at Newborough in Staffordshire, not many miles from Foston, and died in 1717, leaving one son.

A thousand thanks to my dear Mrs. Eyre for the best orange I ever tasted. I should have bought your lute-string, but as you said you were in no hurry I was in hopes they might grow cheaper, for I never knew silks so dear as this spring. I sent you a cap, by Wilkins, and Mrs. Manroi's bill, and desired you would let me know if it was right, for as she has not been in England this year I would not pay it for fear of a mistake. We will settle accounts when we meet, and your gown shall be given to your matua-maker in three or four days. I have a worse cold and hoarseness than ever I had in my life. To cure it I went to Windsor for a few days, and am returned better, though not well; however I hope to be with you at Derby the last week in this month, if that time is agreeable to you and Mr. Eyre (to whom I beg my compliments), and that you will let me hear from you as soon as possible. My stay with you will be not so long as I could wish, because I have promised to pass some time with Mrs. Egerton at Foston.

I have so many things to do that I must bid you adieu, and only add that I am

Most sincerely yours,

J. COKE.

Saville Row, May the 9th, 1754.

Mr. Meynell has been with me this morning.

LETTER XXX.

I have been so much out of order since I wrote last to dear Mrs. Eyre that I have kept my room for some days. However, I hope I am now much better, and hope nothing will prevent my setting out for Derbyshire on Monday the 27th of this month, whither I shall make three or four days, I have not yet resolved, but you shall know whether to expect me the Wednesday or Thursday. I shall trouble your house with no other servant but my own maid. I have bought your gown and sent for your mantua-maker, and shall order it to be an open sack and flounced sleeves. Mrs. Manroi I will pay, and we'll settle accounts when we meet. Adieu, dear Mrs. Eyre, believe me,

Yours affectionately,

J. COKE.

Saville Row, May 17th, 1754.
My compliments to Mr. Eyre, etc.

LETTER XXXI.

Lady Jane is back in London again after a month's visit to Derbyshire, and is congratulating herself upon having accomplished the tedious journey safely, and without mishap. The "Great Bashaw" is her nickname for Mr. Eyre, from whom she speedily receives an unexpected letter.

I am, my dear Mrs. Eyre, safely seated in my own easy chair without having met with any accident, or even a fright in my journey. My first thought was, how much I was obliged to you for the agreeable time I passed in Derbyshire, but I am too much hurried to say half what I think on the subject, either to you or the rest of my neighbours. I own it pleased and flattered me extremely to find myself so kindly remembered by them all; even the "Great Bashaw" was good to me; pray tell him I think so, and my best compliments attend him. I had no reason to complain of the heat of the weather, which was stormy and gloomy, but when I came within ten miles of London 'twas very dusty. I go to Windsor on Sunday evening; from thence you shall hear from me, for at present I've only time to add my kindest compliments to Madam Sal:, and assure dear Mrs. Eyre, I am her

Most affectionate and obliged,

J. COKE.

My best and kindest wishes always attend Mrs. Cotton and her family.

Saville Row, June the 28th, 1754.

P.S.—As I am engaged all to-morrow I write this the day before the post goes, and to my great surprise have just received a letter from Mr. Eyre, which I will answer very soon. Amongst all his faults I never thought I should have called him flatterer.

LETTER XXXII.

This allusion to Mrs. Eyre's sister Katherine Cotton's entanglement is the first intimation we have of her subsequent marriage to Mr. Shirley, afterwards Lord Ferrers, to which her relations were very much opposed on account of that family's idiosyncracies.

The reader will remember that in the postscript to Letter XXIV. Lady Jane says that Lady Caroline

Harpur's match is denied by all her friends in London. However, we now see that Mrs. Eyre's information was quite correct, and that the widow Lady Caroline Harpur is now Lady Caroline Burdett, having in the meantime become the second wife of Sir Henry Burdett of Foremark. The Duchess of Montrose was a sister of Lady Caroline Burdett, being also a daughter of John, second Duke of Rutland, and James her only son was born on the eighth of February, 1755, and afterwards became the third Duke of Montrose.

The Duchess of Hamilton and Lady Coventry were, as mentioned in Letter XV., the daughters of John Gunning, Esquire of Castle Coote. Their mother was a daughter of Viscount Bourke of Mayo. The eldest of the two celebrated beauties, Maria, married George William, the sixth Earl of Coventry, in March 1752, and the youngest, Elizabeth, married first in February, 1752, James, the sixth Duke of Hamilton, and secondly in 1759 Colonel John Campbell, afterwards the fifth Duke of Argyll, for whom she had refused the Duke of Bridgewater. The Duchess of Hamilton and Argyll was the mother of two Dukes of Hamilton and two Dukes of Argyll. These ladies are both very frequently mentioned by Horace Walpole. In 1752 he writes, "The two Miss Gunnings and a late extravagant dinner at White's are twenty times more the subject of conversation than the two brothers (Newcastle and Pelham) and Lord Granville. These are two Irish girls of no fortune, who are declared the handsomest women alive. I think their being so handsome and both such perfect figures is their chief excellence, for singly I have seen much handsomer women than either; however, they can't walk in the park, or go to Vauxhall, but such mobs follow them that they are generally driven away," and again in 1752, "The great event which has made most noise since my last is the extempore wedding of the youngest of the two Gunnings, who have made so vehement a noise. Lord Coventry, a grave young lord, of the remains of the patriot breed, has long dangled after the eldest, virtuously with regard to her virtue, not very honourably with regard to his own credit. About six weeks ago Duke Hamilton, the very reverse of the Earl, hot, debauched, extravagant and equally damaged in his fortune and person, fell in love with the youngest at the masquerade, and determined to marry her in the spring. About a fortnight since, at an immense assembly at my Lord Chesterfield's, made to show the house which is really magnificent, Duke Hamilton made violent love to her at one end of the room, while he was playing Pharaoh at the other. However, two nights afterwards being left alone with her, while her mother and sister were at Bedford House, he found himself so impatient that he sent for a parson. The doctor refused to perform the ceremony without licence or ring: the Duke swore he would send for the Archbishop. At last they were married with a ring of the bed-curtain at half-an-hour after twelve at night, at Mayfair Chapel. The Scotch are enraged, the women mad, that so much beauty has had its effect; and what is most silly, my Lord Coventry declares that he will now marry the other."

Somewhat later in the same year, Walpole writes about the visits of these two sisters to Yorkshire (referred to in this letter) as follows:—"The Gunning's are gone to their several castles, and one hears no more of them, except that such crowds flock to see the Duchess of

Hamilton pass, that several hundred people sat up all night in and about an inn in Yorkshire to see her get into her postchaise next morning."

Derby China was already becoming known, and well thought of; Glover in his History of Derby says, "The business of porcelain manufacture, was established in Derby 1750 by Mr. Duesbury. It was superior to any other, for the finish and taste of the execution, and obtained great celebrity. Many magnificent services have been sent from this factory to ornament the palaces of Princes, and the mansions of nobility."

"Sunbury appears to have been formerly a favourite locality for the residence of the gentry, its "sunny" situation on the north bank of the Thames, with its pleasantly situated villas, rendering the spot one of the most attractive in the immediate neighbourhood of London."

Windsor,

September the 7th, 1754.

My dear Mrs. Eyre,

Your two entertaining letters have made me some amends for your long silence, before I received the first I was beginning to accuse you of great laziness, not remembering how much your time was taken up with balls, races and assemblies. We have nothing here that sounds half so gay; I'm sorry for the disagreeable company you met, but when one suffers only for having acted right, there is not much in it, however I think I should have left the ball as you did, since I would always avoid anybody capable of saying what must be shocking. I sincerely wish your sister may keep the promise you say she has made, though not to marry him while Mrs. Cotton lives, seems to imply she intends it some time or other, and if she does, I really shall be too angry to pity her, since he is such a creature, that she has not one of the common excuses most women make for playing the fool. I have been told by a relation of his that they were married, but all this is only between you and I, for it is such a family, that I should dread giving my opinion in anything that concerned them. Sure (even in this age of liberty), Miss Shirley's coming to Derby, so attended was rather extraordinary. Mrs. Vernon I hear, was prevented coming to the Races, by having been overturned; their Ball was far from being crowded.

I think Lady Caroline Burdett does great honour to the matrimonial state, since she is younger and gayer than she ever was in her life. The Duchess of Montrose is with child, and coming from Scarborough. All the world have been at York races, where the two beautiful sisters (the Gunnings), the Duchess of Hamilton, and Lady Coventry made their appearance, but to their infinite surprise were thought mere mortals, and not the handsomest of the race, whether this proceeded from too good or too bad a taste, I shall not take upon me to determine. And 'tis time now for me to thank dear Mrs. Eyre for all the trouble I give her, first the purse-strings do extremely well, and are enough for the present, next if the China plates are approved of by you, I would have a dozen made for breakfast plates, and when they are done sent all together to my house in Saville Row, and I will either order the money to be paid by Wilkins, or to anybody they will order to receive it in town. I am rather impatient, so hope they will not be a vast while before they are finished. The linen from Grayson he will send, and you will be so good as to pay for, and then let me know how our account is. You will receive with this a packet from me in which (as you love a new fashion) is a sack-handkerchief, that I think extremely pretty, and vastly decent, I thought you would not understand the pattern, therefore have had one made. You must have it fitted to your neck, for this was made for me, which is the reason of the muslin being double, as it was too transparent single, it must be put on before the sack, and the strings tie under your arms; pray let me know how you like it. I am so tired with writing, that I can only add my best compliments to Mr. Eyre and Madam Sal: and must not attempt saying anything of myself, only that I have agreed to buy a house at Sunbury, when I write next I will tell you more of it. Adieu my dear Mrs. Eyre,

Believe me, ever yours,

J. COKE.

I wrote to Mrs. Egerton soon after I came here, but have never heard from her.

*LETTER XXXIII.

Miss Cotton *did* marry Mr. Shirley in spite of the disapproval of her mother and all the difficulties placed in her way. The match appears to have turned out much better than her friends anticipated.

Cargoose skins.—The cargoose is the crested grebe, which formerly bred in large numbers on the Shropshire meres, near to which the Combermere Cottons' property was situated, and the skins mentioned most probably came from there.

The Dowager Lady Exeter was Hannah Sophia, daughter and heir of Thomas Chambers, Esq., of Derby, and widow of Brownlow, the eighth Earl, who died on November the 7th of this year (1754).

This was another Royal birthday. Thackeray tells us " New clothes on the birthday were the fashion for all loyal people. Swift mentions the custom several times.

If the King and Queen were unpopular there were very few new clothes at the drawing room."

Lady Dysart was Lady Elizabeth Carteret, daughter of John, the first Earl Granville.

Miss Fitz-Herbert was Catherine who married in 1755 Richard Bateman, Esq., of Hartington Hall, Derbyshire. Mrs. Fitz-Herbert, the mother of Catherine Fitz-Herbert, was the wife of William Fitz-Herbert, of Tissington, who was twice Member of Parliament for Derby.

Saville Row, November 26th, 1754.

Not having been very well when I came to London, and having drunk the Spa-water ever since, has prevented my thanking dear Mrs. Eyre for her letters. As to my affairs at Derby, I am only sorry they give you so much trouble, for I am not in any hurry for the china as I intend it for the country, and the lawyers are so tedious about the Act of Parliament, that I don't know when I shall have completed the purchase. I believe I wrote you word some time ago I had agreed for a house at Sunbury, but the Act must be had before the title can be a good one, and though I think I shall certainly have it, yet I cannot begin to make any alterations till I am sure, and there is a great deal to be done.

I have been in constant expectation of hearing Mrs. Cotton was come to town, and wonder you say nothing of it. I hope she has not changed her resolution, as Etwall must be a very melancholy place for her to pass the winter in. I am most sincerely sorry you have so much uneasiness about Miss Cotton. There was a story that she was going away with Mr. Shirley, but prevented by Mrs. Cotton. Whether this is true or no I dare say she intends to marry him, and reasoning with her upon the subject is to no manner of purpose; the only thing (in my opinion) her friends can do for her, is to get her fortune secured. Be so good to make my compliments and thanks to Lady Cotton for the offer of the cargoose skins, which I shall be extremely glad to have a muff and tippet of, but you do not tell me where to send for them. The Dowager Lady Exeter and her daughters are come to town, and have taken a house in Albemarle Street. She is in very great affluence, and her lord made a very reasonable will.

There was more finery than usual on the Birthday, and Miss Chudleigh danced minuets. It is not the least likely that hoop petticoats will be left off, since nobody (except Lady Dysart) goes without them but in a morning. I'm glad Miss Fitz: is going to be well married. Tell Mr. Eyre I am as ever his most obedient, and that I am sure he shines upon the subject, when he and Madam Fitz-Herbert meet. If I can do anything for you here, I beg my dear Mrs. Eyre will employ her

> Most affectionate and obliged,
>
> J. COKE.

Company is come in or my letter would be longer, but I must add compliments to Madam Sal:.

LETTER XXXIV.

The *Derby Mercury* of December 26th, 1754 states: "This morning was married, at All Saints' Church in this town, the Hon. Robert Shirley, Esq., second brother to the Right Hon. the Earl Ferrers, to Miss Cotton, one of the daughters of the late Rowland Cotton, of Etwall, Esq., an agreeable lady with a large fortune."

Lady Hartington was Charlotte, daughter and heir of the Earl of Burlington and Cork, and Baroness Clifford of Lanesborough in her own right. She married William, Marquis of Hartington, who the year after her decease succeeded his father and became fifth Duke of Devonshire.

Lady Mary Wortley-Montagu writes: "Lady Burlington has made a lucky choice for her daughter. I am well acquainted with Lord Hartington; I do not know any man so fitted to make a wife happy, with so great a vocation for matrimony, that I verily believe if it had not been established before his time he would have had the glory of the invention."

Lady Burlington was the sister of Lady Thanet, and mother of Lady Hartington.

Lord Montford was the Right Hon. Henry Bromley, who had been in 1741 created Lord Montford and Baron of Horseheath. Lady Jane's account of his shocking death agrees with Horace Walpole's, who, however, goes into more details, and says: "He himself, with all his judgment in bets, I think would have betted any man in England against himself for self-murder, yet after having been supposed the sharpest genius of his time, he by all that appears shot himself on the distress of his circumstances; an apoplectic disposition, I believe, concurring either to lower his spirits, or to alarm him . . . he has squandered vast sums at Horseheath and in living. He lost twelve hundred a year by Lord Albemarle's death, and four by Lord Gage's the same day. He asked immediately for the Government of Virginia or the Foxhounds, and pressed for an answer with an eagerness that surprised the Duke of Newcastle, who never had a notion of pinning down the relief of his own or any other man's wants to a day. Yet that seems to have been the case of Montford, who determined to throw the die of life and death on the answer he was to receive from Court, which did not prove favourable." Two months later Walpole writes: "I did not doubt you would be struck with the death of poor Bland. I t'other night at White's found a very remarkable entry in our very—very remarkable wager-book: Lord Montford bets Sir John Bland twenty guineas that Nash outlives Cibber. How odd that these two old creatures, selected for their antiquities, should live to see both their wagerers put an end to their own lives. Cibber is within a few days of eighty-four, still hearty, and clear and well.

Lord Gower, the first Earl, was married three times and had in all nineteen children. He was constituted Lord Privy Seal, and sworn of the Privy Council in 1742, and was twice one of the lords-justice during the King's absence.

Feathered muffs became fashionable about this time.

Sir Henry Every twice contested Lichfield, both in 1754 and 1755, and each time unsuccessfully.

My dear Mrs. Eyre,

I cannot congratulate you on your new relation, but as your sister has not taken the opinion of any of her friends, the best wish for them is, that they may hear nothing of her to make them uneasy.

I hope Mrs. Cotton will come to London; you know when people are unhappy, I always recommend a change of scene, though we have had nothing but melancholy subjects for conversation lately. Poor Lady Hartington was lamented by everybody. Lady Burlington is to have all the children live with her. Lord Montfort's manner of dying is vastly shocking. He supped at White's Coffee House the night before, in the morning sent for a lawyer and read over his will, to which he added a codicil, then went only into the next room and shot himself through the head.

A thousand reasons are given; some say his affairs are extremely embarrassed, and others, that he was apprehensive of an attack of the palsy, and always declared he would not live in the way Lord Gower did. I really am grown so old that I do think the world grows worse than it used to be, but that I may not moralize, and give you the vapours, I will tell you some Bath wit which they say is Miss Chudleigh's character, but I beg you'll read them to Mr. Eyre, and let him guess who they describe.

> A wife, who to her husband ne'er laid claim,
> A mother, who her children ne'er dare name,
> Is this a wonder, more may yet be said,
> This wife, this mother still remains a Maid.

They are reckon'd very pretty; you remember her being still a Maid of Honour, which explains them. I am very sorry you have so much trouble about the china when you've paid for it, I beg I may know how much I am indebted to you. Lady Cotton is very obliging; if at any time she has a tippet to spare, I would not trouble her for a muff. I hope you have got rid of your cold. I never remember such bad weather for so long a time together as we have had this winter. I thank God I keep tolerably well, though I have a sad cold. I know you love to have me say something of fashions, and as my dress is always the same, I am very ill-qualified to speak on the subject. Everybody wears flounced sleeves, and all the sacks are made open, with an apron very full trimmed, and as to the caps, they are the same as last year.

My best compliments to Mr. Eyre, and tell him I believe he has a concealed passion for Blowzabella, or he would not think so much how she passes her time. I hope Madam Sal: will not forget me, and that dear Mrs. Eyre will always believe me

Her most affectionate,

J. COKE.

Saville Row, January the 7th, 1755.

Sir H. Every is much talked of, for the bustle he makes at Lichfield; is there any chance of his succeeding?

LETTER XXXV.

Mrs. Bonfoy. The *name* is mentioned by Horace Walpole some years later in connection with the Devonshire family, as he writes, "I went with the Straffords to Chatsworth, and stayed there four days. There were Lady Mary Coke, Lord Besborough and his daughters, Lord Thomond, Mr. Bonfoy, the Duke, the old Duchess (of Devonshire), and two of his brothers."

Lady Jane had purchased the place known as Sunbury Park, evidently intending permanently to establish herself there, and besides building an addition to the house, it is recorded that she cast longing eyes upon a small eyot in the river Thames belonging to Sir Charles Kemeys-Tynte, and coveted it so much that she gave him in exchange a large picture of Charles I. riding on a dun-coloured horse, by Vandyke, which is now at Halswell in the possession of the Kemeys-Tynte family.

My dear Mrs. Eyre,

I am very sorry you have passed so melancholy a winter. Indeed I had not heard from you for so many months that I was afraid you were not well. I hope Mrs. Cotton is perfectly recovered, and that she will not hear any more of distresses she neither occasioned nor can remove. I have seen poor Lady Curzon, you know it is but four years next June since I saw her, and she is so excessively altered in every respect that she surprised me. She thinks and talks of nothing but her grandchildren. The eldest is inoculated, and in a very good way.

Mrs. Fitz-Herbert is really quite an evergreen, for I think her person and spirits just the same they were when I lived in Derbyshire. She spoke of Mrs. Bonfoy as one thoroughly miserable, but if, as you say, she loves dress and lovers, she may be not quite so much to be pitied.

The Devonshire family are vastly prejudiced against her.

Sir Robert and Lady Caroline Burdett talk of going to the Bath, and so much out of order as they both are, I think them wrong in losing any part of the spring season. I thank God I have had no reason to complain of my health this winter. Sunbury begins to look gay, and I wish myself there. I am building a large room and three servants' rooms. Don't you think it a great undertaking? I quite despair of ever seeing you there. My compliments to Mr. Eyre and Miss Cotton, and believe me, dear Mrs. Eyre, ever

Yours sincerely,
J. COKE.

A thousand thanks for the cheese, which is as good as Parmesan.

March the 26th, 1755.

LETTER XXXVI.

Lady Jane writes of the new spring fashions, "clouded" silks were either watered or shot with darker shades. It was the fashion for children to wear caps, and never forgetful of Madame Sal: she sends her little friend a present of one.

Shops and houses of business were distinguished by signs, as numbers on houses were not introduced until a later period.

Carriers were obliged to carry goods at certain fixed rates, and the tariff at this time between Derby and London was six shillings per hundred weight, and as they chiefly conveyed heavy goods, it appears not to have been safe to entrust them with small and valuable articles.

Thursday, April the 14th.

Dear Mrs. Eyre,

As I go out of town for the summer to-morrow, I have only time to tell you I have seen all the new lute-strings, that three shops produce, those made for this summer are all clouded, I think vastly ugly and dear, for they are all dark colours. In short I would not venture to buy one for you, if I was in your place I would have a plain one, and if you write to Mr. Hinchliffe, mercer at the Hen and Chickens, in Henrietta Street, Covent Garden, and say I recommended you, he will send you some patterns. I send inclosed one of the only striped I've bought for this summer, which I think a pretty one, but I know you dislike yellow, it was bought at Swan and Bucks, mercer at the Wheat and Sheaf in King Street, Covent Garden. Mrs. Dantin the sack-maker lives in Mount Street, near Grosvenor Square; and now as for caps, I have got you one of blonde which I bespoke, and one I intend as a present to

Madam Sal:, but do not know how to send them, 'tis too small to go by the carrier, and yet if they are tumbled they are spoiled, and I have set my heart upon your liking them; pray let me know how they are to be conveyed. Direct your next to me at Sunbury in Middlesex, and believe me

Sincerely yours,

J. COKE.

My compliments to Mr. Eyre, and Madam Sal:, he is very cross not to let you return my visits.

LETTER XXXVII.

Lady Jane alludes to the young lady who was with her; she was probably Miss Anna Maria Draycott, to whom she left her fortune, and who afterwards married George, the second Earl of Pomfret, he subsequently being appointed Lord of the Bedchamber, and ranger and keeper of the little park, Windsor. In 1764 Walpole, writing to Lord Hertford, says "Before I have done with Charles Townshend I must tell you one of his admirable bon-mots. Miss Draycott, the great fortune, is grown very fat; he says her tonnage is become equal to her poundage." In explanation of this jest it must be remembered that the duties of tonnage and poundage were amongst the chief sources of revenue of that time.

I am very much obliged to you, my dear Mrs. Eyre, for your kind inquiry, and thank God I've had no reason to complain of my health all this summer. I can't imagine how the reports could come of my not being well, as there has been no foundation for it. I am most sincerely sorry for the loss of Mr. Meynell; he had sent me some game the week before he died, and wrote a letter in very good spirits. I've heard nothing of his will but what you told me, and think it a pity he did not give his niece a little more.

The weather now begins to put me in mind of London, and I propose going to settle there in about three weeks. I conclude Mrs. Cotton is by this time come to her winter habitation, and hope she is very well. My best wishes always attend her. I think she is very good in taking Mrs. Shirley, and by all I've heard he is of such a disposition, there is no probability of his being ever any comfort or credit to his family. There is certainly something wrong in all those brothers and sisters. The youngest Miss Shirley, since I came from Bristol, took a miserable lodging at Hampton, no mortal with her but one maid, nor any acquaintance to carry her about. She visited the young lady who is with me, and one morning walked hither. It rained, and I asked her to stay dinner, but she would not. Her eldest sister I hear is become a Methodist, and in great favour with Lady Huntingdon. We have dealt extremely in drums this autumn, and would you believe it, I have been at one ball and all the assemblies. Now we are grown very quiet, some of my neighbours gone, and the rest going. Mr. Hodgkinson stays a week longer, which I think much for the credit of Sunbury, as he is rather apt to tire of the country.

I did not wonder to hear of Miss Ward's disposal of herself. If the man has a good character I don't think her friends have any reason to be dissatisfied.

My dear Mrs. Eyre, if you have any commands in London when I go, I beg you will employ

Your most affectionate,
J. COKE.

Sunbury, October 29th, 1758.

My compliments to Mr. Eyre and Miss Cotton.

This is the last of the only four letters that remain to represent the six years that Lady Jane spent at Sunbury before her death, which took place on the 4th of January, 1761, at Bath, whither she had apparently gone for the benefit of her health. According to her desire, thus expressed in her will, " First I desire to be buried in a private manner at Sunbury," her body was conveyed to Sunbury, and interred there on the 15th of the same month.

Walpole remarks that "Lady Jane Coke is dead, exceedingly rich. I have not heard her will yet."

By her will, after bequests to various friends, and substantial legacies to her servants, who appear to have served her faithfully and well, she leaves "all the rest residue and remainder of my estate, both real and personal, and whatsoever and wheresoever, unto Anna Maria Draycott, of Clarges Street, Piccadilly," appointing her sole executrix.

In the Parish Church of St. Mary, Sunbury, on the north wall, is a monument to Lady Jane Coke. It is unfortunately now entirely hidden, and blocked out by a modern organ, and it is impossible to approach near enough to read the inscription, or to obtain any drawing or photograph of it. It appears to be an elaborate marble mural monument. Alas! poor Lady Jane! her memory is not even thus preserved in Sunbury, where she passed the last years of her life, although such was not the intention of her heiress Miss Draycott, afterwards the Countess of Pomfret, who caused this fine monument to be erected to her benefactress as the following shows, which is an exact copy of the inscription, taken from the "Claim to the Wharton peerage" by the Kemeys-Tynte family.

Near this place are interred the remains of the Right Honourable Lady Jane Coke, eldest daughter of Thomas Marquis of Wharton, and Lucy his wife, daughter of Adam Loftus Baron Lisbourne, of the kingdom of Ireland, and sister of Philip, late Duke of Wharton, and the last of that noble family. She first married John Holt, of Redgrave, in the county of Norfolk, Esquire, and secondly Robert Coke, of Longford, in the county of Derby, Esquire, and departed this life the 4th day of January, 1761, aged 54. This monument was erected by Anna Maria Draycott, as the least honour that gratitude could pay to her memory.

THE END.

INDEX.

Act to Prevent Gambling, 40, 106, 110
Actors, Provincial, 40, 42, 116
Aix la Chapelle, 111
Amelia, Princess, 115, 118
Argyll, Duke of, 126
Ashbourne, 40, 90
Assemblies, 27, 29, 42, 67, 161
Assembly, Derby, 90, 91, 111, 116, 122
Assembly Room, Derby, 7, 9, 13
Assembly, Rules of, 8
Aston, Sir Willoughby, 113, 116
Atkins, Sir R., 12, 13, 14
Auretti, The, 65, 68
Babington, Family of, 3, 4
Babington House, 3, 4
Bailey, Miss Kitty, 21, 22, 25, 41, 43
Banks, Miss Peggy, 87, 90
Banks, Robert, 87
Barnes, Mr., 9, 13, 116, 122, 138
Barnes, Mrs., 7, 8, 9, 13, 34, 36, 50, 122, 123, 129, 138
Bath, 62, 63, 76, 94, 95, 118, 124, 129, 157, 161
Bath, Lord, 113
Bath Wit, 154
Bedford, Duchess of, 27, 29, 36, 58
Berkeley, Earl of, 120
Birthday, The, 32, 36, 119, 120, 123, 148, 150
Blenheim, 125, 129
Blowzabella (Mrs. Barnes), 40, 42, 54, 91, 92, 105, 111, 113, 116, 155
Bonfoy, Mrs., 155, 156

Bragg, Game of, 30, 31, 32, 36, 67
Bragg, Verses on, 31, 32
Brand, Mr., 12, 14
Bright, Miss, 71, 72, 75
Bristol, 160
Bristol, Earl of, 102, 103
Brydges, Family of, 69
Brydges, Mr., 69, 74, 113, 116
Burdett, Lady Caroline, 143, 146, 157
Burdett, Sir Henry, 143, 157
Burlettas, 131, 134
Burley House, 51
Burlington, Earl of, 29
Burlington, Lady, 151, 152, 153
Bustles at Derby, 14, 19
Cargoose skins, 148, 150
Carnarvon, Lady, 132, 135
Carnarvon, Lord, 117
Carriers, 158, 159
Cato, Acted by Royal Children, 22, 23, 25
Cattle Plague, 26, 28
Cavendish, Lord Frederick, 86
Chamberlayne, Miss Elizabeth, 63
Chandos, Duke of, 114, 117
Chatsworth, 5, 6
Chudleigh, Miss, 101, 102, 105, 107, 110, 114, 130, 150
Chudleigh, Miss, Verses on, 154
Chudleigh, Mrs., 108, 111
Cibber, Mrs., 37, 42, 64
Cliveden, 85, 89
Cobham, Lady, 76, 83
Coke, Carey, xvii., 133
Coke, Family of, xvi., 63

INDEX.

Coke, Lady Jane, ix., xvi., xvii., xviii., xix., xx., xxi., xxii
Coke, Monument to Lady Jane, xxi., 162
Coke, Portrait of Lady Jane, xviii., xix.
Coke, Lady Mary, 68, 69, 97, 125, 126, 127, 128, 130
Coke, Lady Mary, Lady Temple's lines on, 128
Coke, Rt. Hon. Thomas, 64, 67, 68
Coke, Robert, xvi., xvii., xix., xxi., 14, 19, 37, 43, 44, 45
Coke, Thomas William, xvii.
Coke, Viscount, 68, 97, 125, 126, 130
Coke, Wenman, 66, 68, 73, 86, 130
Coke, Mrs. Wenman, 86, 90, 130
Coke, Will of Lady Jane, 69, 162
Collyer, Lady Caroline, 57
Collyer, Lady Juliana, 93, 94, 95
Conolly, Hon. William, 59, 63
Conolly, Hon. Thomas, 59
Corbet Family, 35
Cornwallis, Lieut.-General, 59
Cornwallis, Mrs., 59, 60, 63, 94, 99, 104
Cotton, Elizabeth Abigail Lady, 2, 73, 76, 150, 154
Cotton, Family of, xviii., 36
Cotton, Hester Salusbury, 2, 3
Cotton, Katharine, 35, 43, 91, 97, 99, 103, 142, 146, 148, 151
Cotton, Mary, xviii., xxiii., 1
Cotton, Mrs., 2, 35, 62, 84, 110, 118, 137, 146, 149, 150, 153, 156, 160
Cotton, Rowland, xxi., 2, 35, 92, 94, 118
Cotton, Sir Lynch Salusbury, 2, 34, 73
Coventry, Lady, 72, 121, 123, 143, 146
Coventry, Lord, 72, 75, 144
Cumberland, Duke of, 86, 87, 124
Cumberland Lodge, 124, 129
Curzon Family, 57
Curzon, Lady, 71, 75, 82, 117, 134, 156

Curzon, Lady Caroline, 61, 65, 71, 75, 93
Curzon, Mr., 57, 61, 65, 115, 117
Curzon, Sir Nathaniel, 57, 61, 71, 82, 115, 117
Curzon, Viscount, 115
Dartmouth, Earl of, 113
Delaval Blake, 131, 134
Denmark, Queen of, 92, 93
Denmark, Mourning for the Queen of, 95
Derby, xiv., 3, 7, 9, 12, 13, 14, 18, 19, 20, 21, 22, 25, 40, 42, 45, 50, 55, 75, 76, 86, 91, 94, 96, 105, 113, 115, 122, 130, 137, 140, 149, 151
Derby China, 145, 147, 149
Derby Races, 9, 50, 55
Devonshire, Duke of, 5, 86
Donington Park, 16
Dorset, Duchess of, 120
Dorset, Duke of, 58, 120
Dovedale, 88, 90
Draycott, Anna Maria (Countess of Pomfret), xxi., 159, 162, 163
Drayton, 120, 121
Drumlanrig, Earl, 58
Drury Lane, 134
Egerton, Mrs., 53, 56, 139, 140, 148
Egremont, Lord, 58, 61
Egginton, 21
Election at Derby, 18, 19
Election, Derbyshire, 86, 90, 91
Election and Scrutiny, 39, 40, 42
Etwall, xxi., xxiii., 1, 31, 45, 104, 128, 150
Etwall Hall, xxii., 1
Every, Mr., 21, 25
Every, Sir Henry, 21, 153, 155
Exeter, Daughters of Lord, 58, 61
Exeter, Dowager Lady, 148, 150
Eyre, Family of, xxii., xxiii., xxiv.
Eyre, Gervase, xxiv.
Eyre, Mr. (Henry), xxii., 2, 3, 14, 20, 25, 42, 55, 61, 68, 84, 88, 89, 92, 99, 111, 116, 118, 135, 138, 140, 141, 142, 150, 154, 155, 159

INDEX.

Eyre, Mrs., xviii., xxi., xxii., 1, 2, 3, 6, 34, 96
Eyre, Miniature of Mrs., xxiii.
Farce, New, at Drury Lane, 64, 67
Fashions, 43, 55, 79, 80, 83, 111, 123, 132, 134, 135, 147, 155, 157, 158
Ferrers, Baroness, 71
Ferrers, Countess, 7
Ferrers, Earl, 16, 35
Ferrers, Lady, 58, 61, 71, 75, 113, 122
Ferrers, Laurence Earl, 114, 117
Ferrers Sewallis, Earl, 142
Ferrers, Selina Lady, 82, 84
Fireworks, 9, 10, 11
Fitz-Herbert, Catherine, 149, 150
Fitz-Herbert, Family of, 18
Fitz-Herbert, Mr. John, 40, 42
Fitz-Herbert, Mr., 93, 95
Fitz-Herbert, Madam, 149, 151
Fitz-Herbert, Mrs., 18, 20, 156
Fitzwilliam, Earl, 27, 28, 29, 52, 72
Finch, Anne, 51
Finch, Edward, 50, 51
Finch, Lady Mary, 52
Finch, Mr., 50, 51, 56
Finch, Mrs., 101, 104
Finch, William, 51
Foston, 53, 140
Franceys, Mr., 8
French Ambassadress, 33, 34, 36, 43, 83
French Players, 38, 39, 42
Furnese, Lady Anne, 81, 84
Furnese, Sir R., 82, 106
Gambling, 42, 63, 64, 67
George II., 70, 74, 92, 93, 95, 107
Germain, Lady Betty, 120, 123
Goodwyns, x.
Gower, Earl, 58, 153, 154
Guildford, Earl of, 106, 124, 128, 129
Guildford, Lady, 106, 109, 112, 134
Gunnings, The, 72, 75, 121, 143, 144, 146
Hamilton, Duchess of, 143, 145, 146

Hamilton, Duke of, 72, 102, 107, 143, 144
Hamilton, Lady Anne, 107, 110
Hampton, 160
Hartington, Lady, 151, 152, 153
Hartington, Lord, 86, 90, 151
Harpur, Elizabeth, xxii.
Harpur, Lady Caroline, 118, 119, 143
Harpur, Sir Henry, 118
Hastings, The Ladies, 16
Hervey, Lieut. Augustus John, 102 103
Hodgkinson, Mr., 87, 90, 95, 112, 161
Holkham Hall, 68
Holt, Family of, xv.
Holt, John, xv.
Holt, Lord Chief Justice, xv.
Huntingdon, Countess of, 15, 16, 17, 20, 110, 161
Huntingdon, Earl of, 16
Hulse, Sir Edward, 97, 99
Inoculation, 108, 156
Installation at Windsor, 100, 104
Journey from London to Derby, 96, 98, 140, 141
Kedleston, 57, 61, 65, 68, 71, 82
King of France, 57, 60
Kingston, Duchess of, 103
Kingston, Duke of, 12, 58, 93, 95, 100, 101, 102, 103, 105, 110, 130
Kirby Hall, 51
Knights of the Garter, 100
Lamb, Mr., 64, 67
Lee, Anne, xi.
Leicester, Earl of, xvii., 68, 73, 125
Lewison, Lady Betty, 58, 61
Lichfield, 153, 155
Longford, xvi., xix., 15, 24, 62, 66, 84, 129, 130
Longford Hall, xvii., xviii., 3
Lovell, Baron, 60, 68
Lovell, Miss, 60, 63
Lute-string, 139, 158
Marlborough, Duke of, 85, 86, 90, 100, 120, 125

INDEX.

Marlborough, Sarah, Duchess of, x., 120
Massarene, Earl of, xxiii., 115
Massarene, Lady, 115
Melbourne, 64, 65, 68
Melbourne, Viscount, 64
Methodists, 16, 17, 110, 160
Meynell, Mr., 40, 43, 75, 111, 140, 160
Meynell, Mr., Anecdote of, 41
Meynell, Family of, 41
Mirepoix, Madame de, 33, 34
Mirepoix, Marquis de, 33
Mobb, 1
Montagu, Lady Mary Wortley, xv., 12
Montford, Lord, 152, 153
Monkey Island, 85, 90
Montrose, Duchess of, 143, 146
Morice, Sir William, xii.
Morice, Lady Lucy, xii.
Murray, Fanny, 12, 13, 14
Nash, Beau, 8, 107, 110
Nash, Beau, verses on, 107
Niccolina, The, 131, 134
Nicholl, Frances, 113, 114, 117
Nicholl, Margaret, 80, 84, 114, 117
North, Lord, 106
Northumberland, Lady, 132, 135
Okeover, Family of, 65, 68, 83
Okeover, Leake, 65, 91
Okeover, Mrs., 65, 80, 84, 114, 117
Operas, 67, 134
Orford, Margaret, Countess of, 81, 84, 87
Orford, Lord, 80, 84, 114
Orkney, Lady, 85, 89
Oxford, 129
Peak District, xxiii., 24, 25, 92
Pelham, Henry, 121
Pelham, Miss, 121, 123
Petersham, Lady Caroline, 101, 121, 123
Pierpont, Lady Caroline, 12, 14
Plays, 64, 134
Pole, Family of, 5, 6, 134
Pomfret, Earl of, 159
Pomfret, Countess of, xxi., 162

Pomfret, Lady, 120
Portmore, Earl of, 57, 93
Pulteney, Lord, 113, 117
Queen Mother, 121, 123
Queensberry, Duke of, 58, 61
Radbourne, 5, 6, 24, 25, 105
Ranelagh, 77, 78, 79, 83, 96, 98
Redgrave, xv.
Rivet, Thomas, 18, 22, 25
Rivet-Carnac, Sir James, 22
Roach, Miss, 48, 54
Roads, Country, 15, 20, 24, 28, 128
Robbing in the Streets, 23, 24, 25
Roberts, Major Philip, xvii.
Roberts, Wenman, xvii., 63
Rockingham Castle, 52, 53
Rockingham, Lady, 52, 56, 57, 60, 75
Rockingham, Marquis of, 27, 52, 71, 72, 75
Routs, 136, 137
Rowtor, xxiii., xxiv., 89
Rowtor Hall, xxiv.
Rutland, Duke of, 33, 118
St. Albans, Duke of, 113, 117
St. Werburgh's, Derby, 9
Sal:, Madam, 2, 34, 35, 55, 68, 73, 99, 111, 118, 122, 124, 155, 157, 159
Sackville, Lady, 58, 61
Savile Row, 29, 74, 116
Scarborough, 118, 146
Scarborough Waters, 119
Scarsdale, Baron, 35, 57, 115
Seymour, The Ladies, 33, 36
Shirley, Hon. Sewallis, 81, 84
Shirley, Family of, 72, 73, 142, 146, 160
Shirley, Miss, 58, 62, 76, 95, 117, 146, 160
Shirley, Mr., 148, 150, 151
Shirley, Mrs., 153, 160
Shirley, Rev. Walter, 58, 72, 75, 95
Sibley, Miss, 22, 25
Silks, Expense of, 61
Sinfen, Moor, 50
Skipwith Mrs., 69, 74, 82

INDEX.

Sleigh, Family of, xxii.
Sleigh, Sir Samuel, xxii., 35
Smallpox, 97, 99, 108, 110
Stanhope, Edwin Francis, 133, 135
Stanhope, Hon. John, 9, 13, 18
Stanhope, Sir William, 3, 4
Stanhope, Thomas, 18
Stomachers, 122, 123
Stowe, 76, 77, 83, 116
Sudbury, 124, 131
Sunbury, xxi., 145, 148, 149, 156, 157, 159, 161, 162
Sunbury Park, 149
Thanet, Earl of, 58, 61, 68
Thanet, Lady, 152
Thanksgiving Day, 12
Theatre, The Little—in the Haymarket, 38, 42, 67
Touche, Madame de la, 93, 95, 105
Townshend, Audrey Lady, 15, 16, 20, 71, 114
Townshend, Augustus, 59
Townshend, Lady, 71
Townshend, Marquis, 15
Townshend, Rt. Hon. Charles, 15
Townshend, Viscount, 15, 58, 59, 71, 75, 98
Trentham, Lord, 39, 42
Truelove, xxiii.
Tufton, Lady Mary, 68
Tunbridge Wells, 46, 47, 48, 53, 67, 106, 109, 110
Tynte, Sir Charles Kemeys, 156
Vane, Lady, 48, 49, 54, 81
Vane, Lord, 48, 49, 54
Vauxhall, 77, 78, 79, 83, 87, 96, 98
Vernon, Henry, 59, 62
Vernon, Mrs., 131, 134, 146
Vernon, of Sudbury, 124, 128, 131
Virginia Water, 124, 129
Waldgrave, Colonel John, 58, 61
Wales, Frederick, Prince of, 69, 70, 74, 85, 89
Wales, Death of Frederick, Prince of, 70, 74

Wales, Mourning for Frederick, Prince of, 79, 83, 95
Wales, George, Prince of, 71
Wales, Princess of, 28, 29, 32, 70, 74, 101, 119
Walpole, Family of, 59
Ward, Family of, 6
Ward, Miss, 130, 161
Ward, Mrs., 6, 90
Waters, Effect of taking Mineral, 46, 53, 62, 67, 109, 119, 149
Watson, Mrs., 121, 123
Wesley, 16, 17, 20
Wharton, Duchess of, xii., xiv.
Wharton, Maria Theresa, Duchess of, xiv., 69, 74
Wharton, Duke of, xi., xii, xiii, xiv., xvi., 69, 74, 119, 122
Wharton, Family of, ix.
Wharton, Marchioness of, xi., xv., xvi.
Wharton, Marquis of, x., xi., xvi.
Wharton, Lady Lucy, xii.
Wharton, Lady Jane, xii., xv., xvi.
Wharton Portraits, xi., 80
White's Coffee House, 153
Whitefield, 16, 17
Willoughby, Elizabeth, xxii.
Willow, Wearing the, 22, 25, 43
Wilmot, Rev. Robert, 18, 20
Wilmot, Mrs., 18, 20, 95.
Winchelsea, Lady, 101, 104
Winchelsea, Lord, 51, 52, 56
Winchenden, x.
Windsor, 82, 89, 92, 94, 96, 99, 100, 104, 109, 116, 117, 129, 130, 138
Windsor, Pope's lines on, 97
Windsor Forest, 82, 124
Wooburn, x., xi.
Wroxton Priory, 106, 124
Wyville, Sir Marmaduke, xvii., 133, 135
Yarmouth, Lady, 27, 28, 29
York Races, 146

O

Demy 8vo.—Cloth Extra.—10s. 6d.

CAMPING AND TRAMPING IN MALAYA
BY
AMBROSE B. RATHBORNE.

The first impression produced by this book is that of the author's thorough-going acquaintance and familiarity with his subject. This was gained during fifteen years' exploring and surveying of pathless tracts of forest, swamp, and mountain, and thereafter laying down excellent roads, those sure engines of civilization. Evidently, too, he combined great powers of endurance with a keen faculty of observation, and with a humane forbearance and sympathy with the natives. Altogether the book is an acceptable contribution to the literature of a region about which too much has not yet been written, and on the political and social development of which Englishmen may look with legitimate pride.—*Athenaeum*, 8/10/98.

A substantial contribution to our knowledge of the native states of Malaya, and still more as offering, to stay-at-home English people, a refreshing dip into a region still little known and as foreign morally as geographically.—*Speaker.*

Mr. Ambrose Rathborne has many qualifications for the task of acting as guide to this part of the Asiatic Dominions of Great Britain, and it may be safely said that no Englishman will rise from a perusal of this book without having obtained a clearer view both of the country and the people who inhabit it than he had before, and without, at the same time, having acquired an added respect for those unostentatious heroes of peace, who, quite as much as the soldier and the statesman, are building up the fabric of Empire.—*Times.*

He is an excellent and assiduous observer, fair-minded and sympathetic, and we cannot mention any book from which one could get a better idea of life in a tropical jungle, where, under the influence of British rule, favoured by the existence of enormous undeveloped mineral wealth, peace and security have been established among a number of tribes, native and immigrant, of very diverse character, and extraordinary progress made in industry and civilization.—*Manchester Guardian.*

Mr. Rathborne has supplied a well-written and entertaining volume regarding a country which offers many advantages for settlements, and which is now being rapidly developed under the guidance of British officials. Numerous photographic views appear throughout the text, which add to the interest of the work.—*Journal of the Royal Colonial Institute.*

A delightfully informative book concerning a territory and peoples as to which and whom comparatively little has hitherto been written. The author has a thorough knowledge of the country.—*Liverpool Post.*

Most of the special qualities that go to make up a thoroughly interesting, instructive, and enjoyable narrative of travel combine together to delight the reader in this most attractive volume. The manner too in which Mr. Rathborne relates his many adventures contributes in no small degree to the charm of this book. It is simple and straightforward, unmarred by any straining effect or unique self-consciousness on the part of the author. In short, from whatever point of view the volume be considered, there is nothing in it but deserves the most cordial praise.—*Glasgow Herald.*

LONDON: SWAN SONNENSCHEIN & CO., LIM.

WILLIAM BYLES & SONS, PRINTERS, 129, FLEET STREET, LONDON
AND BRADFORD.

www.ingramcontent.com/pod-product-compliance
Lightning Source LLC
Chambersburg PA
CBHW032227230426
43666CB00033B/1631